# RELIGIOUS CONFLICT IN FOURTH-CENTURY ROME

## A Documentary Study

# SOURCES IN ANCIENT HISTORY
*General Editor*: E. A. Judge, Macquarie University

This series is designed to provide translations of substantial bodies of source material with accompanying discussion particularly suitable for tutorial use by students of ancient history or of political and social institutions.

# RELIGIOUS CONFLICT IN FOURTH-CENTURY ROME

A Documentary Study

Brian Croke & Jill Harries

 SYDNEY UNIVERSITY PRESS

SYDNEY UNIVERSITY PRESS
Press Building, University of Sydney

UNITED KINGDOM, EUROPE, MIDDLE EAST, AFRICA
Eurospan Limited
3 Henrietta Street, London WC2E 8LU

NORTH AND SOUTH AMERICA
International Scholarly Book Services, Inc.
P.O. Box 1632, Beaverton, OR 97075, U.S.A.

National Library of Australia Cataloguing-in-Publication data

Croke, Brian
     Religious conflict in fourth-century Rome.

     Bibliography.
     Includes index.
     ISBN 0 424 00091 1.

     1. Church history — 4th century — Sources. 2. Rome —
     Religion — Sources. 3. Rome — Politics and government —
     284-476 — Sources. I. Harries, Jill. II. Title. (Series:
     Sources in ancient history).

  200'.901

First published 1982
© Brian Croke and Jill Harries 1982

Printed in Australia by Macarthur Press (Books) Pty Limited, Parramatta

# Contents

## PROLOGUE: THE ETERNAL CITY

### (A) Ammianus Marcellinus on Rome

### (B) Claudian on Rome

### (C) The Conversion of Rome

#### (i) Prudentius

#### (ii) Paulinus of Nola

## CHAPTER 1: EMPERORS AND PAGANISM FROM CONSTANTINE TO THEODOSIUS

### (A) Edicts Establishing Christianity

#### (i) 'Edict of Toleration', AD 311

## (ii) 'The Edict of Milan', AD 313

# (B) Letters of Constantine

# (C) Anti-Pagan Legislation

## CHAPTER 2: THE DEBATE ON THE ALTAR OF VICTORY, AD 384

## CHAPTER 3: REACTION AND REVIVAL, AD 392-4

## CHAPTER 4: ANTI-PAGAN POLEMIC

---

## CHAPTER 5: CHRISTIAN AND PAGAN ARISTOCRATS AT ROME

### (A) Quintus Aurelius Symmachus
#### (i) Inscription

#### (ii) Letters of Symmachus

### (B) Vettius Agorius Praetextatus and Fabia Aconia Paulina
#### (i) Inscriptions

## (C) Nicomachus Flavianus

### (i) Inscription

### (ii) Letters of Symmachus

## (D) Sextus Petronius Probus and Anicia Faltonia Proba

### (i) Inscriptions

(ii) Letter of Symmachus

## (E) Ambrose

Letters of Symmachus

---

# Preface

The fourth century AD was a period of religious diversity and intense theological and philosophical conflict on issues that have attracted increasing interest in recent years. Our purpose in this book is, therefore, the modest one of collecting together in annotated translation much of the material relevant, both directly and as background, to the debate between pagan and Christian aristocrats in the city of Rome in the late fourth century. The documents are presented in such a way as to illuminate (at the risk of exaggerating their contemporary importance) two major incidents that encapsulate the issues involved — the petition to restore the Altar of Victory to the senate-house in 384, and the public revival of pagan ceremonies during the reign of the usurper Eugenius in 394. At the same time we have endeavoured to build into our presentation of the documents the results of recent research on the many diverse aspects they embody, while leaving the interpretation of the documents to the reader. Our aim is to raise questions rather than to answer them. Although the book is designed primarily for use by students at school and university, we hope it will be of wider interest in that it offers a collection of material on a popular theme, a good deal of which is here made available in English for the first time.

Inevitably, this volume is limited in scope. It makes no attempt to embrace the full diversity of fourth-century religious life, pagan and Christian; nor the nature and complexity of doctrinal controversy; nor the shifting balance of power between church and state, bishop and emperor; nor the process of Christianization outside the city of Rome. That would require a book of an altogether different complexion.

The fourth century is an era rich in documentation and selection from it has not been easy. We have confined ourselves to sources deriving from, or relating to, the Latin West. We have therefore excluded such major writings from the Greek East as the anti-Christian works of the emperor Julian and of Libanius, the orator of Antioch. Although we have taken Rome as the focal point, some of the writers included originate from elsewhere in Italy, as well as Gaul, Spain and Africa. We have tried to offer instances of different aspects of the controversy — legislative, political, social and literary — under the separate chapter headings. However, these facets are to a large extent interdependent and the chapter divisions are, therefore, to some degree arbitrary: for example the laws of Theodosius I occur in Chapter 1 but are also fundamental

to Chapters 3 and 4, and assertions of a Christian Rome are as
at home in the Prologue on the 'Eternal City' as in Chapter 4 on
anti-pagan polemic. Our choice of 410 as the terminal date was
dictated by the revolutionary change in the terms of the debate
caused by the sack of Rome by the Visigoths in that year.

In writing this book we have been encouraged by the interest
and advice of several people and wish to thank in particular Alan
Cameron, Edwin Judge, John Matthews, John Richardson and the
Oxford research seminar on Pagans and Christians held in Trinity
term, 1976.

**Brian Croke**
**Jill Harries**

# Abbreviations

| | |
|---|---|
| CCh | Corpus Christianorum |
| CIL | Corpus Inscriptionum Latinarum |
| Cod. Theod. | Codex Theodosianus |
| CSEL | Corpus Scriptorum Ecclesiasticorum Latinorum |
| GCS | Die griechischen christlichen Schriftsteller |
| ILS | Inscriptiones Latinae Selectae |
| MGH AA | Monumenta Germaniae Historica. Auctores Antiquissimi |
| PL | J.-P. Migne (ed.), Patrologia Latina |
| PLRE I | A. H. M. Jones, J. Martindale and J. Morris, The Prosopography of the Later Roman Empire, vol. I, Cambridge 1971 |
| PLRE II | J. Martindale, The Prosopography of the Later Roman Empire, vol. II, Cambridge 1980 |

# Table A: Dates of Emperors and Events

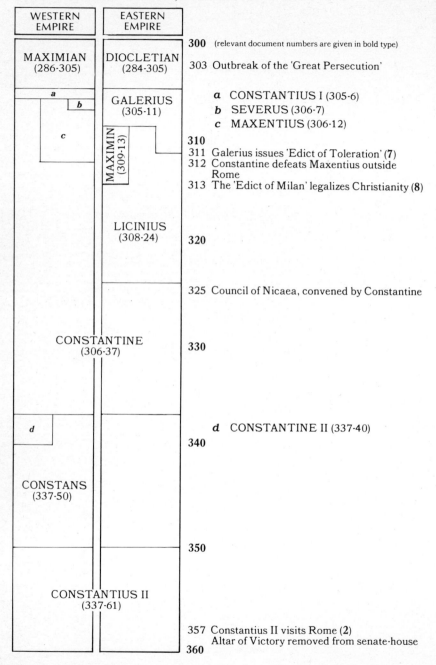

| WESTERN EMPIRE | EASTERN EMPIRE | |
|---|---|---|
| | | **300** (relevant document numbers are given in bold type) |
| MAXIMIAN (286-305) | DIOCLETIAN (284-305) | 303 Outbreak of the 'Great Persecution' |
| *a* | GALERIUS (305-11) | *a* CONSTANTIUS I (305-6) |
| *b* | | *b* SEVERUS (306-7) |
| *c* | MAXIMIN (309-13) | *c* MAXENTIUS (306-12) |
| | | **310** |
| | | 311 Galerius issues 'Edict of Toleration' (**7**) |
| | | 312 Constantine defeats Maxentius outside Rome |
| | | 313 The 'Edict of Milan' legalizes Christianity (**8**) |
| | LICINIUS (308-24) | **320** |
| | | 325 Council of Nicaea, convened by Constantine |
| CONSTANTINE (306-37) | | **330** |
| *d* | | *d* CONSTANTINE II (337-40) |
| | | **340** |
| CONSTANS (337-50) | | |
| | | **350** |
| CONSTANTIUS II (337-61) | | |
| | | 357 Constantius II visits Rome (**2**) Altar of Victory removed from senate-house |
| | | **360** |

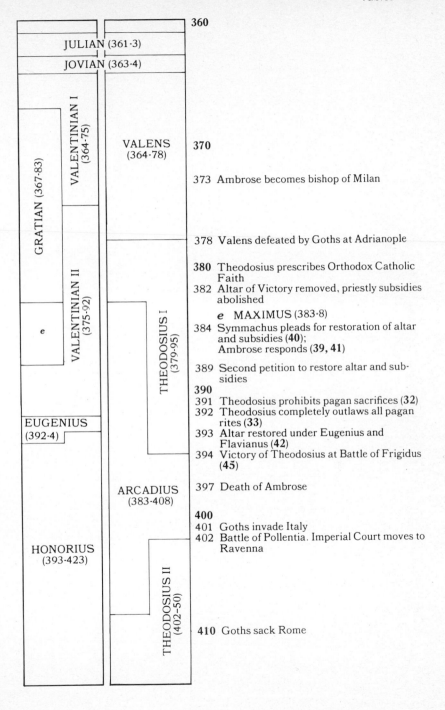

360

JULIAN (361-3)

JOVIAN (363-4)

GRATIAN (367-83)

VALENTINIAN I (364-75)

VALENS (364-78)

370

373  Ambrose becomes bishop of Milan

378  Valens defeated by Goths at Adrianople

380  Theodosius prescribes Orthodox Catholic Faith

382  Altar of Victory removed, priestly subsidies abolished

VALENTINIAN II (375-92)

e

THEODOSIUS I (379-95)

e  MAXIMUS (383-8)

384  Symmachus pleads for restoration of altar and subsidies (**40**); Ambrose responds (**39, 41**)

389  Second petition to restore altar and subsidies

390

391  Theodosius prohibits pagan sacrifices (**32**)

392  Theodosius completely outlaws all pagan rites (**33**)

EUGENIUS (392-4)

393  Altar restored under Eugenius and Flavianus (**42**)

394  Victory of Theodosius at Battle of Frigidus (**45**)

ARCADIUS (383-408)

397  Death of Ambrose

400

401  Goths invade Italy

402  Battle of Pollentia. Imperial Court moves to Ravenna

HONORIUS (393-423)

THEODOSIUS II (402-50)

410  Goths sack Rome

# Table B: The House of Valentinian and Theodosius

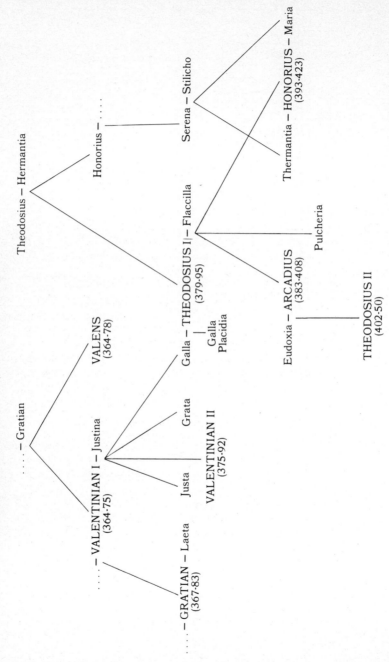

# Prologue:
## THE ETERNAL CITY

By the opening of the fourth century AD, Rome was no longer the seat of government of the Roman Empire. The need for an emperor to travel, to see and be seen by his subjects in the provinces, had drawn emperors like Hadrian away from Rome even in the second century. By the third century, the constant menace of barbarians on the northern — Rhine and Danube — frontiers had made the emperor's presence there essential. The administrative capital was where the emperor was, and several cities could claim an imperial residence: Trier in Gaul, Sirmium on the Save (a tributary of the Danube), Milan in Northern Italy. Diocletian at the end of the third century established himself at Nicomedia in Bithynia and, in 330, Constantine formally founded Constantinople as the counterpart of Rome in the East.

Yet the mystique of the ancient capital remained. It was the seat of the Senate which was a reservoir of administrative experience, of economic power through the senators' extensive landed properties, and of intellectual awareness. Over the centuries, Rome had acquired buildings that were not only visually beautiful but, to the lover of tradition, symbolically potent. This was especially true of the temples and shrines that made Rome a natural stronghold of the old pagan state religion, in particular the 'Capitoline triad' of Jupiter*, Juno* and Minerva*. It was this environment that produced the most articulate defender of late Roman paganism, the senator, orator and letter-writer, Q. Aurelius Symmachus, for whom Rome was not simply 'Roma' but the 'urbs aeterna', the Eternal City.

Rome was similarly a stronghold of Christianity. The Roman Church had been founded on the blood of the martyrdoms of Peter and Paul and the bishop of Rome was pre-eminent among the bishops of the West. The Roman Church was both the oldest and the richest in martyrs and monetary endowments. For all the Christians of the Empire the conquest of Rome by Christianity was

---

* An asterisk in the text refers the reader to an entry under that name in the 'Glossary of Deities and Rites' (pp.126–31).

equivalent to the conquest of the world.

The following extracts illustrate the views of Rome held by her admirers, pagan and Christian.[1]

## (A) AMMIANUS MARCELLINUS ON ROME

Ammianus, a 'former soldier and a Greek', as he described himself, probably came from the Latin-speaking upper classes of Antioch in Syria. He wrote a history in Latin in thirty-one books of which only the last part, from Book XIV onwards, is extant. He wrote in Rome in c. 390 after having served in his early career as *protector domesticus*, a member of the emperor's military entourage, on the Eastern frontier and in Gaul in the reigns of Constantius II and Julian. The history covers much of his period of active service from 353 to 378. He was a pagan but tolerant of the Christian religion, reserving criticism for individuals, on the whole, rather than groups.[2]

---

### Document 1: Ammianus, *Res Gestae* (History) XIV.6.3-6

(3) When Rome was first rising to universal splendour to live as long as man endures, Virtue and Fortune, normally in disagreement, made a pact never to be broken, that Rome might grow to pre-eminence; for, if one or other quality had been lacking, she would not have reached the highest point of supremacy. (4) Her people from the cradle to the end of childhood, a period of about three hundred years, sustained warfare around their own walls; then, on entering upon adulthood, they crossed the Alps and the sea after many hard-fought wars; growing into full manhood and middle life, they brought back triumphal laurels from every part of the entire world; and now, turning towards old age, victorious often by her name alone, she has settled into a quieter existence. (5) Thus, after making the proud necks of savage tribes bow beneath the yoke and making laws to be the foundation and anchor of freedom for all time, the honoured city, like an honest parent who is both circumspect and rich, has given up her family estate to the management of the Caesars, as she would to her own children. (6) And, although

---

1.  For a detailed discussion of the attitudes of individual Christians and pagans to Rome see F. Paschoud, *Roma Aeterna: Etudes sur le patriotisme romain dans l'occident latin à l'époque des grandes invasions*, Rome-Bern 1967.
2.  On this important historian see E. A. Thompson, *The Historical Work of Ammianus Marcellinus*, Cambridge 1947 (repr. Groningen 1969) and, for his intellectual and religious culture in particular, P. M. Camus, *Ammien Marcellin. Témoin des courants culturels et religieux à la fin du iv$^e$ siècle*, Paris 1967.

the tribal assemblies are at rest and the centuriate assembly pacified, and there is no struggle for votes, as the tranquillity of Pompilianus' time is with us once again,[3] nevertheless all the lands and regions of the world accept her as mistress and queen, the authority and experience of the Senate are everywhere respected, the name of the Roman people well-regarded and revered.

## Document 2: Ammianus, *Res Gestae* (History) XVI.10.13-17

(13) Then Constantius, upon entering Rome [in 357], the hearth of sovereignty and all excellence, and reaching the rostra, the most famous seat of power from ancient times, stood in amazement, overwhelmed by the wonderful sights which crowded upon him on all sides wherever he looked. In the senate-house he addressed the nobility, and from the tribunal the people, and was welcomed to the palace with many demonstrations of favour, enjoying a pleasure he had long awaited. When giving equestrian games, he was frequently delighted by the witty heckling from the crowd who neither presumed too far nor fell short of their traditional freedom of speech, while he also respected convention. (14) For he did not, as in other cities, allow the games to finish whenever he chose but let them run their usual course as circumstances decided. Then, as he took in the parts of the city bounded by the seven hills, the slopes and the level ground in-between, as well as the suburbs beyond, he presumed whatever first met his eye dwarfed all the rest; the sanctuaries of Tarpeian Jupiter* which surpass all others as the divine surpasses the things of this earth; baths built out to the size of provinces; the massive Amphitheatre with its strong frame of Tiburtine stone, the top of which is almost as far as the eye can see; the Pantheon, like a rounded city-quarter in itself with its high and beautiful vaulting; and the lofty pinnacles with stairs to their decks and bearing images of previous emperors; and the Temple of the City, the Forum of Peace, the Theatre of Pompey, the Odeon, the Stadium and other ornaments of the Eternal City.[4] (15) But when he came to the Forum of Trajan, a construction without equal on earth, so we believe, which even the gods deem marvellous, he halted in astonishment,

3.   During the period of the Roman republic the people were assembled regularly and arranged according to tribes (*comitia tributa*) and centuries (*comitia centuriata*) for the purpose of passing laws and electing magistrates. These assemblies gradually ceased to function under the empire. Numa Pompilius was the legendary second King of Rome, the successor of Romulus, and was credited with the introduction of religious ceremonies and laws (Livy I.18-21).

4.   For the location and remains of these buildings: E. Nash, *A Pictorial Dictionary of Ancient Rome*, Rome 1961; S. Platner and T. Ashby, *A Topographical Dictionary of Ancient Rome*, Rome 1965; and P. Bigot, *Rome antique au iv⁵ siècle après J·C*, Paris 1955.

spreading his gaze around the massive structures which defy description and will never again be reached by mortal man . . . (16) . . . When
Ormisda⁵ was asked what he thought of Rome, he said that his only
consolation was that he had learned that even here men were mortal.
(17) So having reviewed many amazing and awe-inspiring sights, the
emperor complained that Rumor* must be weak or spiteful because,
while always exaggerating everything else, she is feeble when it
comes to describing the wonders of Rome.

## (B) CLAUDIAN ON ROME

Claudius Claudianus came from Alexandria to the imperial court
in 394 to become first the panegyrist of the senatorial Anicii, but
later, and chiefly, the propagandist of Honorius' minister, Stilicho,
whose policy he consistently justifies in his poetry. He died probably between 404, the date of his last poem, and the murder of
Stilicho in 408. Although he deals with Christian topics he is
believed to have been a pagan, and is labelled as such by Augustine
and Orosius.⁶

Document 3: Claudian, *De consulatu Stilichonis* (On the Consulship of Stilicho) III.130-73

As Consul, you are all but equal of the gods, since you are
guardian of this mighty city, loftier than all on the face of the earth.
No eye can absorb its size, no mind can grasp its splendour and
no voice is adequate to praise it; shining with gold her heights reach
up to rival the neighbouring stars, (135) her seven hills mirror the
seven regions of heaven. Mother of military and legal might, she
spreads her rule over all men and was the cradle of Justice from
its infancy. This city it is which sprang from narrow bounds to extend
from pole to pole, and setting out from her modest foundation (140)
spread her power in the wake of the sun. When this city was exposed
to Fate, while simultaneously fighting countless battles on several
fronts, taking control of Spain, blockading the towns of Sicily, laying
low Gaul by land and Carthage by sea, she never gave way to her
losses, nor was she cowed by any wound, but roared all the more

5.    Ormisda, more commonly Hormisdas, was a Persian prince in exile at the
      Roman court who accompanied the emperor Julian on his Persian expedition
      in 363 ('Hormisdas 2', *PLRE* I, p. 443).
6.    Augustine, *De Civitate Dei* (City of God) V. 26, copied by Orosius VII.35.31.
      The standard work on Claudian is Alan Cameron, *Claudian: Poetry and Propa-
      ganda at the Court of Honorius*, Oxford 1970.

fiercely after the disasters of Cannae and Trebia;[7] (145) when the flames were already upon her and the enemy [Hannibal] battering her very walls, she sent an army against farthest Spain.[8] At the Ocean she did not halt but launched her galleys on the deep and sought out the Britons in another world to conquer them.[9] She is alone in welcoming the vanquished into her embrace (150) and, in the manner of a mother and not a mistress, sheltered the human race under one and the same name; and those she has conquered she calls her citizens and unites remote lands in a bond of duty. To her peaceful ways we all owe it (155) that a foreigner may regard each region as his homeland; that he can change his abode; that it is just a game to visit Thule[10] and explore its once terrifying, secluded corners; that everywhere we may drink of the Rhone, taste the waters of the Orontes;[11] that we are all one people.

Nor shall there ever be set a limit (160) to the sway of Rome; for luxurious vice and hateful pride overthrew all other empires. So Sparta shattered the misplaced haughtiness of Athens but succumbed herself to Thebes; so the Medes robbed the Assyrians of rule (165) and the Persians the Medes; Macedonia conquered Persia but was herself to give way to Rome.[12] This city was strengthened by the prophecies of the Sibyl* and given life by the sacred rites of Numa*. For her, Jupiter* shakes his thunderbolt and Tritonia* covers her fully with her Gorgon shield. Here Vesta* brought her secret torches, Bacchus* his rites (170) and the tower-crowned mother [Cybele*] her Phrygian lions. With his gliding motion a guest from Epidaurus slid into this city to cure disease and thus the island on the Tiber gave shelter to the Paeonian Serpent* after his journey across the sea.

---

Document 4: Claudian, *De sexto consulatu Honorii* (On the Sixth Consulship of Honorius) 39-52

This city, and no other, truly deserved to be the home of the rulers of the world. (40) On no other hill [i.e. the Palatine] can civil power hold its head so high, knowing that this is the pinnacle of supreme law; the Palace towers above the rostra at its feet. How numerous are the surrounding shrines it sees, with what divine protection is she embraced! What joy to see below the temple of the

---

7.   The reference is to Roman defeats in the Second Punic War at the hands of Hannibal in 216 BC (Cannae) and 218 BC (Trebia).
8.   The Roman counter-offensive in Spain under the Scipios lasted, with mixed success, from 218 to 206 BC.
9.   Caesar invaded Britain in 55 and 54 BC but the island was not annexed before the expedition of the emperor Claudius in AD 43.
10.  A name used to symbolize the remotest of lands.
11.  A river in Syria, here symbolizing the easternmost parts of the empire.
12.  Standard moralizing on the rise and fall of empires.

Thunderer [Jupiter*], (45) the Giants suspended from the Tarpeian Rock, the carved doors, the statues hanging in a shroud of mist, the many temples piled to the sky, the bronzes attached to pillars adorned with many prows of ships, the sanctuaries resting on massive crags, (50) the work of man crowning that of nature, and the countless arches blazing with their trophies of victory. Sight is bewildered by the shining of metal and falters, blinded by the overwhelming gold.

# (C) THE CONVERSION OF ROME

## (i) Prudentius

The Christian poet Aurelius Prudentius Clemens (348-c.408) came from the Ebro valley in north-east Spain. In early life he was an advocate and governed provincial cities in some capacity, before being raised to a position close to the emperor himself. He retired to devote himself to the writing of Christian poetry in c. 395. The *Peristephanon* (or 'Crowns of the Martyrs'), a collection of fourteen poems written at different times on Spanish and other martyrs, was included in his 'collected edition' published in 404-5, but the Laurence poem probably dates from the 390s, before the poet's pilgrimage to Rome.[13]

Document 5: Prudentius, *Peristephanon* (On the Crowns of the Martyrs) II.1-20, 413-564

Lines 1-20

Rome, the former mother of temples but now given over to Christ, under Laurence's leadership[14] you have prevailed and triumph over barbarians' rites. You had already subdued proud kings, reined in nations and now you impose on monstrous idols the yoke of your empire. One glory alone among all her prizes (10) the city of the toga lacked, to conquer foul Jupiter* by the taming of savage pagan-

13.  An accessible introduction to Prudentius is V. Edden, 'Prudentius' in J. Binns (ed.), *Latin Literature of the Fourth Century*, London 1974, pp. 160-82.
14.  St Laurence, a deacon of the church at Rome, was executed in the persecution following the edict of Valerian against Christians in AD 258. Pope Damasus (366-84) founded a basilica to the martyr which became a focal point for aristocratic piety. Since Prudentius had probably not yet visited Rome or seen the basilica the poem may be contrasted with *Peristephanon* XI (Hippolytus) and XII (Ss. Peter and Paul) which are clearly eye-witness reports of the buildings and cults.

ism, a glory won not by the mere brute strength of a Cossus, a Camillus or a Caesar[15] but by the not unbloody struggle of the martyr Laurence. Faith fought under arms and did not spare her own blood; for by death she destroyed death (20) and for her own sake sacrificed herself.

[As chief deacon at Rome, Laurence is ordered by the Prefect of the City to surrender to him the wealth of the Church. He responds by collecting all the poor and crippled of the city who received charity from the Church and displaying them to the Prefect as the true wealth of the Church, arguing that the souls of the poor were pure and rich in heavenly things while the rich are corrupted by lust for money. Laurence is duly tortured and finally roasted on a gridiron, from which he makes a prayer for Rome as the future Christian city.]

Lines 413-536, 553-64

'O Christ, the one name, splendour and strength of the Father, creator of heaven and earth, guardian of these walls, you have placed Rome's sceptre supreme over all things, ordaining that the world shall serve the toga of Quirinus [i.e. Roman rule] and (420) submit to her armies, so that you could tame the habits and practices, speech, character and worship of disparate peoples under one system of laws; see how all mankind has passed to the kingdom of Remus and, although unlike in their practices before, now shares the same language and beliefs. This was resolved so that (430) the rule of the Christian name might all the more bind all lands together with a single bond. Grant, Christ, the prayer of your Romans that the city through which you have brought all into a single religion may be Christian. All members of the empire are henceforth allied in the one creed. The conquered world is growing peaceful; (440) peaceful too let its capital be. Let her see her separated regions join us in one state of grace. Let Rome's founder, Romulus, become a member of the faith and Numa himself become a believer. The Trojan aberration[16] still confuses the senate of Catos, and honours at secret hearths the Phrygians' exiled deities.[17] Two-faced Janus* and Sterculus* (450) — I shudder to name so many of the fathers' monstrosities — and old Saturn's* festal day are worshipped by the senate. Wipe out this shame, O Christ. Send down your servant, Gabriel,

15. Cornelius Cossus triumphed over the town of Veii in 428 BC, an important step in Rome's rise to power in Italy (Livy IV.19-20). Camillus led the Roman resistance to the Gallic invasion of 390 BC while Caesar was responsible for the subjugation of Gaul.
16. According to Roman legend Aeneas brought his gods to Italy from his native Troy. Virgil's *Aeneid* described the story for educated Romans.
17. A reference to the cult of Cybele*.

so that blind and straying Iulus[18] may recognize the true God. We possess already the most trustworthy pledges of that hope, for already the two princes (460) of the apostles [Peter and Paul] reign here, the one who summoned the gentiles, the other who occupies the foremost throne and opens up the gates of eternity which are in his charge. Away with you, adulterous Jupiter*, defiled by incest with your sister, leave Rome to be free and flee her people who are now Christ's. Paul casts you from our bounds; (470) Peter's blood banishes you and Nero's deed hurts you, his armourer.[19] I foresee that in the future there shall come an emperor [Theodosius I], a servant of God, to forbid Rome to be a slave to shameful abominations of religious rites, to close and bar the temples, lock the ivory doors, destroy the cursed entrances, (480) barring them with bolts of brass. Then at last shall marble shine clean and unstained with blood, the bronzes now seen as idols shall stand purified of guilt.'[20]

His prayer ended and with it his bondage to the flesh; his spirit broke out eagerly when his speech was done. (490) Some senators whom the martyr's amazing freedom had persuaded to follow Christ raised his body and carried it on their shoulders. The spirit [i.e. of Laurence] suddenly penetrated their inmost hearts and induced them to reject former frivolities for the love of God on high. From that day, the worship of shameful gods waned: fewer people gathered at their shrines (500) while there was a rush to the judgement seat of Christ ... (509) That death of the holy martyr was in truth the death of the temples, and Vesta*, powerless, saw the Palladian Lares* safely abandoned. Those Romans formerly accustomed to pray at Numa's cup[21] now throng the halls of Christ which re-echo with the martyr's name in hymns. The very men who were the senate's pride, formerly priests of the Lupercal* or flamines,[22] (520) fondly kiss the thresholds of the apostles and martyrs. Illustrious families, men and women of noble birth, dedicate their high-born children with prayers before our eyes. A priest who once wore the headbands of pagan ritual is marked with the sign of the Cross and into your own church, Laurence, there enters a Vestal, Claudia.[23]

Three, four, even seven times blessed (530) is the resident of Rome who at close quarters pays honour to you and the dwelling-place where your bones rest; he is permitted to kneel close by and weep tears upon the place, press his breast to the ground and quietly

18. Son of Aeneas and ancestor of Romulus.
19. Nero launched his persecution of the Christians at Rome after the disastrous fire in AD 64.
20. The preservation of works of art was compatible with the outlawing of paganism. See Document 35, p. 25.
21. A reference to the rites associated with Numa*.
22. The flamines were a group of priests responsible for the maintenance of a particular public cult. There were fifteen such cults at Rome.
23. A well-known Vestal Virgin who became a Christian ('Claudia 4', PLRE I, p. 206).

pour out his prayers ... (553) Admitted to heaven as a citizen of the indescribable city, on the citadel of the immortal senate you, O Laurence, wear the civic crown.[24] I picture the martyr shining with precious jewels, (560) he whom heavenly Rome has elected a perpetual consul. The power entrusted to you, the magnitude of the duty given you, is displayed in the rejoicing of the [Roman] citizens whose petitions you grant.

## (ii) Paulinus of Nola

A senatorial aristocrat of Aquitanian parentage, Paulinus of Nola was governor (*consularis*) of Campania in 381, but in about 389 experienced a violent conversion to ascetic Christianity. By 395, he had surrendered his property and become a priest at Nola. Poem XIX, one of an annual series in honour of St Felix of Nola, was composed for that saint's 'birthday' on 13 January 405.[25]

Document 6: Paulinus of Nola, *Carmen* (Poem) XIX.45-75

Since the all-healing Lord wished to deliver us from these ills, he provided for us frail mortals in our sickness holy physicians with healthful piety scattered through the various nations; and, so as to make more clear the concern shown by the divine power, he granted them to the more powerful (50) cities, although small towns kept certain martyrs ... (53) Then he put Peter and Paul in the city of Rome because the capital of the world, being driven insane by her many vices and blinded by her darkness, needed the chief doctors. Yet because the power of God is greater to restore our salvation than to keep men imprisoned still in the wiles of Satan, the darkness of the world decreases (60) and holiness prevails almost everywhere and life has conquered death. As the faith grows stronger, error is overcome and will fall away, and, with hardly anyone left in the power of evil and death, all Rome acknowledges the name of Christ and mocks Numa's* fantasies and the Sibyl's* prophecies. (65) Among the numerous flocks of the supreme God the devout crowd responds to the holy shepherds with a glad Amen. The sacred cry strikes to heaven with praises of the eternal Lord and the pinnacle of the Capitol totters with the shock. The neglected images in the empty temples tremble (70) when struck by the pious voices, and

24. The notion of celestial citizenship and civic crowns was a traditional one at Rome. For details: J. Préaux, 'Caeli Civis', *Mélanges J. Heurgon*, Paris 1976, II, pp. 825-43.
25. For Paulinus of Nola: W. H. C. Frend, 'The Two Worlds of Paulinus of Nola' in Binns, *Latin Literature*, pp. 100-33; C. H. Coster, 'Paulinus of Nola' in his *Late Roman Studies*, Cambridge, Mass. 1968, pp. 183-204; and the standard work, P. Fabre, *Saint Paulin de Nole et l'amitié chrétienne*, Paris 1949.

are overthrown by the name of Christ. Terrified demons abandon their deserted shrines. The envious Serpent[26] pale with rage struggles in vain, his lips blood-stained, bemoaning with his hungry throat the redemption of man, and at the same time now, with unavailing groans, (75) the predator writhes around his dry altars cheated of the blood of sacrificial cattle.

26.  As part of the *taurobolium**, a ritual slaying of a bull in the cults of Cybele* and Mithras*, a snake was represented as licking up the blood on the altar (L. Campbell, *Mithraic Iconography and Ideology*, Leiden 1968, pp. 15 ff.).

# Chapter 1

# EMPERORS AND PAGANISM FROM CONSTANTINE TO THEODOSIUS

For the first three centuries of its existence, Christianity was viewed by the Roman state with a distrust which, on occasions, broke out into active hostility. The new religion which seemed initially no more than an heretical offshoot of Judaism differed, like Judaism, from other religions of the normally tolerant Roman Empire in its exclusivity and its denial of all gods but its own. In an era when the survival of the Roman state was generally believed to depend on the favour of its gods the Christian refusal to sacrifice could be seen as bringing down divine wrath on the Empire — in the form of plagues or military disasters. In times of crisis the Christian minorities, with their strange 'love-feasts' held in graveyards in the middle of the night and other secret practices, were natural scapegoats and thus became the objects of persecution by several emperors.[1] This culminated in the 'Great Persecution', begun in 303 under Diocletian (284-305) and prosecuted vigorously by his successor Galerius (305-11) down to 311.[2] Memories of the persecutions were preserved into the fourth century in the cults and Acts of martyrs and church historians: thus, paradoxically, those executed by agents of the Roman state were com-

---

1. For adverse views of Christianity in the second and third centuries see the contemporary attempts to counteract these views: Minucius Felix, *Octavius* (translated, with excellent commentary, by G. Clarke in the series *Ancient Christian Writers*, vol. 39, New York 1974, and also by G. Rendall in the Loeb Classical Library); Tertullian, *Apology* (trans. T. Glover in Loeb Classical Library); and Arnobius of Sicca, *The Case Against the Pagans* (trans. G. McCracken, *Ancient Christian Writers*, vols 7 and 8, New York 1949). Some relevant extracts can also be found in N. Lewis and M. Reinhold, *Roman Civilization. Sourcebook II: The Empire*, New York 1966, pp. 584-9.
2. The fullest general account of the persecutions is W. H. C. Frend, *Martyrdom and Persecution in the Early Church*, Oxford 1965. Contemporary accounts can be found in H. Musurillo, *The Acts of the Christian Martyrs*, Oxford 1972. There are some relevant documents in Lewis and Reinhold, *Roman Civilization*, pp. 591-601.

memorated and venerated by a church that, in the fourth century and after, had the full support and protection of the laws of the state.

## (A) EDICTS ESTABLISHING CHRISTIANITY

## (i) 'Edict of Toleration', AD 311

The 'Great Persecution' ended in April 311 with the promulgation by Galerius on his deathbed of the so-called 'Edict of Toleration', a document preserved in Greek in the *Church History* of Eusebius, Bishop of Caesarea, writing under Constantine; and in the original Latin by his North African contemporary, Lactantius, in a polemical treatise vindicating the anger and power of the Christian God.[3]

---

Document 7: Lactantius, *De mortibus persecutorum* (On the Deaths of the Persecutors) 34

Among other measures that we have constantly promulgated for the advantage and benefit of the state, we had previously desired to set right all matters related to the Romans, in accordance with the ancient laws and discipline of the state and to make such provision that even Christians who had abandoned the religion of their forebears should return to their right senses. For, by some means or other, so strong a spirit of self-will had possessed these same Christians and such stupidity had seized them that they refused to follow the principles of the men of old, which their own ancestors had perhaps been the first to establish, but rather chose to make rules for themselves to observe according to their own judgement and as they saw fit, and to hold meetings of various people in different places. Finally, when our order was published that they should betake themselves back to the traditions of men of old, many were subjected to persecution and many even brought to disaster. But since the majority have persisted in their vocation and we observe that they neither offer the worship and religious observances due to the gods, nor do they respect the god of the Christians, we believed it right in consideration of our most merciful clemency and in view of our perpetual custom of granting pardon to all men, that we should offer our promptest indulgence to these people too, namely that they should be entitled to exist as Christians again and

---

3.  For the thought and background of Lactantius see R. Ogilvie, *The Library of Lactantius*, Oxford 1979, and for Lactantius as an historian of Constantine, T. D. Barnes, 'Lactantius and Constantine', *Journal of Roman Studies*, 63, 1973, pp. 29-46.

set up their places of meeting, provided they do nothing to con-
travene public order. Moreover, in another letter we will indicate
to the governors what they should observe. Wherefore, in accordance with this indulgence of ours, they shall be expected to pray
to their god for the safety of ourselves and of the state, as well as
their own, that the state may continue secure on every side and
that they may be able to live securely in their own homes.

## (ii) 'The Edict of Milan', AD 313

In October 312, Constantine overthrew his rival for empire,
Maxentius, at the Milvian Bridge outside Rome, and established
himself as sole ruler of the West. In 313, he and his Eastern colleague Licinius agreed at Milan that there should be complete freedom of worship throughout the empire: the so-called 'Edict of
Milan' that survives appears to have been a directive to provincial
governors, and hence the honorific titles 'Your Devotion' etc.

Document 8: Lactantius, *De mortibus persecutorum* (On the
Deaths of the Persecutors) 48.2-6

When I, Constantine Augustus and I, Licinius Augustus, happily
met together at Milan and discussed every matter pertaining to the
advantage and security of the state, in addition to the other measures
that we have perceived would be beneficial to most of mankind,
we believed that there should be promulgated a law in support of
reverence for the divine, namely this: that we grant to Christians and
to all others full permission to follow whatever religion they please,
so that whatever divinity exists in the celestial seat may be pleased
and propitious towards us and all under our rule. Therefore we resolve with salutary and most upright reason that this course should
be followed, namely that it is our view that opportunity of worship
should not be denied to anyone who wishes to devote himself to
the observance of the Christians or to that religion which he feels
most suited to him, in order that the Supreme Divinity, whose
worship we follow with free hearts, should in all things afford us
his favour and goodwill. Wherefore it is right that Your Devotion
should know that it is our pleasure that all provisions on the subject
of Christians contained in letters previously sent to your office, which
seemed entirely perverse and alien to Our Clemency, be entirely
removed, and that now each individual among them who holds the
aforesaid wish to practise the Christian religion should freely and
without interference hasten to do so without encountering anxiety
or annoyance to himself. This measure we saw fit to communicate
to Your Solicitude in full, so that you should be aware that we have
given free and unconditional freedom of worship to these same

Christians. And while you will perceive that this grant has been made to them by us, Your Devotion is also aware that a like power of religious observation or worship has likewise been made available and free also to others, in accordance with the peace of our rule, so that each man should have the right to worship freely, in the manner of his own choosing. This we have done so that we should not detract from any mode of paying honour or worship.

[There follow regulations on restoration of places of assembly to Christians without compensation to those who bought them or received them as gifts. This is to apply to property of both individuals and churches, and their restoration is the governor's responsibility. The governor is also charged with publishing the decree.]

# (B) LETTERS OF CONSTANTINE

With the accession of Constantine, and his conversion to Christianity, the once persecuted sect became an object of imperial favour and patronage. Eusebius recorded significant aspects of the growth of the wealth and legal privileges of the Church by including copies of several documents in the last book of his *Church History*.[4]

Document 9: Eusebius, *Historia Ecclesiastica* (Church History) X.5.15-17 (Constantine to Anullinus, proconsul of Africa, 313)[5]

5. 'Greetings to you, most esteemed Anullinus. It is characteristic of our benevolence to desire that whatsoever rightly belongs to another should not only not suffer damage, but should be restored, most esteemed Anullinus. Wherefore we desire that, whenever you should receive this letter, all things belonging to the Catholic Church of the Christians in any city or other place which are now in the private possession of citizens or of anyone else should

4.   Eusebius was the pioneer of the genre of ecclesiastical history, characterized by the extensive quotation of original documents. For details of Eusebius' life and literary output: D. S. Wallace-Hadrill, *Eusebius of Caesarea*, London 1960, and F. J. Foakes-Jackson, *Eusebius Pamphili. A Study of the Man and his Writings*, Cambridge 1933, and for this section of his history: R. M. Grant, *Eusebius as Church Historian*, Oxford 1980.
5.   'Anullinus 2', *PLRE* I, p. 78. Anullinus was involved in the early stages of the Donatist challenge to the legitimacy of Caecilian's episcopate at Carthage.

be restored immediately by you to the aforesaid churches, since we are resolved that all previous possessions of these churches should be given back to them as of right . . .'

---

## Document 10: Eusebius, *Historia Ecclesiastica* (Church History) X.6.1-3 (Constantine to Caecilian, bishop of Carthage, 313)[6]

'. . . I have sent letters to Ursus,[7] the very distinguished financial officer of Africa, and indicated to him that he must be sure to pay to Your Constancy three thousand *folles*. You, for your part, on taking delivery of the above-mentioned sum of money, must issue instructions that this money be distributed to all people listed above[8] according to the list sent you by Hosius.[9] But if you discover that it is in some way too little for you to carry out my purpose with regard to all these recipients, you must not hesitate to request whatever you find is needful from Heracleides,[10] the procurator of our estates . . .'

---

## Document 11: Eusebius, *Historia Ecclesiastica* (Church History) X.7.2 (Constantine to Anullinus, proconsul of Africa, 313)

'. . . I desire that in the province entrusted to you all those in the Catholic Church over which Caecilian presides, who offer service to the holy worship — who are usually denominated as clerics — should be granted exemption and freedom, once and for all, from compulsory public duties,[11] so that they shall not be drawn away

---

6.  The authority of Caecilian as bishop of Carthage was challenged by a rival party, the Donatists, on the ground that he had been consecrated by a bishop who during the Great Persecution had surrendered sacred books to the imperial authorities. After two Church Councils his authority was upheld by Constantine. On the Donatists: W. H. C. Frend, *The Donatist Church. A Movement of Protest in North Africa*, Oxford 1952.
7.  'Ursus 2', *PLRE* I, p. 988. At the time of this letter Ursus was a *rationalis* in Africa. He later became a deputy Praetorian Prefect (*vicarius*) in the West.
8.  Precisely who is being referred to here is not clear from the letter. It must have been a schedule of clerics eligible for this assistance.
9.  Hosius, from Cordoba in Southern Spain, was a most influential adviser of Constantine on ecclesiastical matters.
10. 'Heraclides 2', *PLRE* I, p. 417. This is the only known reference to him.
11. Compulsory public duties (*munera*) primarily involved the holding of municipal offices and magistracies which could involve an individual in great expenses. To be exempted from this burden was a considerable privilege.

by any deviation or sacrilege from the worship that is due to the divinity, but shall devote themselves without interference to their own law. For it seems that, rendering the greatest possible service to the Deity, they also most benefit the state.'

## (C) ANTI-PAGAN LEGISLATION

Other edicts to the same end were included in the *Codex Theodosianus* (Theodosian Code). This is a collection of imperial edicts issued during the fourth and early fifth centuries in the form of instructions to named officials or groups. The Code was compiled by the order of the emperor Theodosius II (408-50) and published in 438 in both halves of the empire. The edicts are grouped by subject matter, with most of those dealing with the Christian religion falling in Book XVI.[12]

Document 12: *Cod. Theod.* XVI.2.2. Constantine Augustus to Octavianus, governor (*corrector*) of Lucania and Bruttium[13]

Those who offer religious service to the divine worship, that is those who are denominated as clerics, are to be exempted entirely from all compulsory public service,[14] lest through the sacrilegious jealousy of certain people they be seduced away from the divine service. 21 October 319.

Document 13: *Cod. Theod.* XVI.2.4. Constantine Augustus to the People

Every man, upon his death, shall have freedom to leave what he wishes of his possessions to the most holy and most venerable assembly of the Catholic Church. These testaments must not be made void. No man is due any greater thing than this, that the writing of his last wishes, after which he can wish for no more, should be free and that the decisions which cannot be repeated should be under no compulsion. 3 July 321.

12. For an introduction to the circumstances of the compilation of the Code, and for a well-indexed translation of the whole Code: C. Pharr *et al.*, *The Theodosian Code*, Princeton 1952, repr. New York 1969.
13. 'Rufinus Octavianus 5', *PLRE* I, p. 638.
14. See n. 11 above. This law represents an extension of this exemption originally granted to the African clergy only.

Document 14: *Cod. Theod.* IV.7.1. Constantine Augustus to Hosius[15]

Those who with pious mind grant deserved freedom to their dear slaves in the lap of the Church shall be held to have made this grant by the same legal right as that by which Roman citizenship . has customarily been granted with the proper legal formalities: but such freedom we resolve should be granted only to those who manumit in the presence of a bishop. However, we grant this additional privilege to clerics that, whenever they grant freedom to their own domestics, they shall be deemed to have given the complete enjoyment of freedom not only when they do so in the sight of the Church and its devout congregation, but also when they manumit in a last will, or give instructions for it to be done by any form of words, so that freedom may be granted immediately from the day of publication of the will, without any witness of the proceeding or legal advice.[16] 18 April 321.

Many of these privileges and exemptions were extended and consolidated in the course of the reigns of the successors of Constantine, although the emphases in their policies varied. The imperial sanction attracted the patronage of many of the wealthy and powerful to the expanding Church. Parallel with this there appeared a series of imperial edicts aimed at limiting and finally prohibiting pagan religions, rituals and sacrifices. These laws applied not only to the state cults but to practices on the fringes of recognized religious ritual, namely the use of divination, astrology and magic.

Document 15: *Cod. Theod.* IX.16.2. Constantine Augustus to the People

We forbid soothsayers, priests and the usual ministers of such rites to approach a private house or cross the threshold of another under pretext of friendship. Should they disregard this law, there is a statutory punishment. Those of you who consider this of benefit to you may go to the public altars and shrines and celebrate your accustomed rites: for we do not prohibit the rites of a past superseded practice from being celebrated openly. 15 May 319.

15. See n. 9 above.
16. The medieval interpretation of this law brings out the point that clerics, unlike others, do not require the presence of a bishop to validate manumission.

## Document 16: *Cod. Theod.* IX.16.3. Constantine Augustus and Caesar (Crispus? Constantine II?) to Bassus, Prefect of the City[17]

The knowledge of those who, being equipped with magic arts, are discovered to have plotted against men's lives or who have perverted modest minds with lust must be punished and a penalty rightly exacted under the harshest of laws. However, exemption from criminal charges should be allowed for cures sought for infections of the human body and the aid innocently invoked in country districts to allay fears of rain falling on the ripe grape harvest or of its being shattered to pieces by destructive hailstorms, seeing that nobody's safety or reputation is harmed thereby, but rather such measures ensure the prevention of harm to both the divine gifts and the labours of men. 23 May, between 317 and 324.

## Document 17: *Cod. Theod.* XVI.10.1. Constantine Augustus to Maximus[18]

If it should be determined that part of our palace or other public building has been struck by lightning, let the ancient custom of observance be retained, as to the portent, and its meaning be investigated by the soothsayers and let the documentary evidence be most carefully compiled and brought to Our Wisdom. Others too are to be granted the freedom to practise this custom, provided that they refrain from domestic sacrifices, which are explicitly forbidden. Let me inform you, moreover, that the official report and interpretation of the striking of the amphitheatre, about which you wrote to Heraclian, tribune and Master of the Offices, has reached us. 17 December 321.

## Document 18: *Cod. Theod.* XVI.2.5. Constantine Augustus to Helpidius[19]

Since we have learned that certain ecclesiastics and others serving the Catholic sect are being compelled by men of different

17.  'Septimius Bassus 19', *PLRE* I, p. 157. Bassus was Prefect of the City of Rome from 15 May 317 to September 319. For a discussion of the problem in establishing these dates: A. Chastagnol, *Les Fastes de la Préfecture de Rome au Bas-Empire*, Paris 1962, pp. 70-1.
18.  'Valerius Maximus Basilius 48', *PLRE* I, p. 590.
19.  'Helpidius 1', *PLRE* I, p. 413. He was Vicar of the City of Rome at the time.

religions to celebrate lustral sacrifices, we decree hereby that whoever should consider that those who serve the most sacred law may
be forced into celebrating the rites of an alien superstition, he shall
be beaten with clubs in public, provided his status so permits. However, if the consideration due to honourable rank protects him from
such injury, let him undergo the penalty of a very heavy fine, which
shall be vindicated to the public funds. 25 May 323.

## Document 19: *Cod. Theod.* XVI.10.2. Constantius Augustus to Madalianus, deputy of the Praetorian Prefect[20]

Let superstition cease. Let the madness of sacrifices be exter-
minated; for if anyone should dare to celebrate sacrifices in violation
of the law of our father,[21] the deified Emperor, and of this decree
of Our Clemency, let an appropriate punishment and sentence
immediately be inflicted on him. Received in 341.

## Document 20: *Cod. Theod.* XVI.10.3. Constantius and Con-stans Augusti to Catullinus, Prefect of the City[22]

Although all superstition must be utterly rooted out, we nevertheless decree that temple buildings located outside the city walls
should remain intact and unviolated. For since some plays, circus
spectacles and athletic contests originate from these temples, it is
not expedient to tear down places where the traditional amusements
of the Roman people are celebrated. 1 November 342.

## Document 21: *Cod. Theod.* XVI.10.4. Constantius and Con-stans Augusti to Taurus, Praetorian Prefect[23]

We have resolved that, in all places and in every city, temples
are to be closed forthwith and that, by forbidding them access, all

20. 'Lucius Crepereius Madalianus', *PLRE* I, p. 530.
21. No such law of Constantine survives.
22. 'Aco Catullinus Philomathius 3', *PLRE* I, pp. 187-8. He was a well-known
    pagan and his daughter married Vettius Agorius Praetextatus (see Documents
    65, 66, 67).
23. 'Flavius Taurus 3', *PLRE* I, pp. 879-80. There is a problem of dating here.
    Taurus must have received this law while Praetorian Prefect of Italy and
    Africa (356-61) but it is dated to a consulship of Constantius II and Constans
    in 346. The normal and most likely solution is that 'Constans' is a mistake
    for 'Julian' so that the law was actually issued in a consulship of Constantius
    and Julian in 356, that is during Taurus' prefecture.

abandoned men are to be denied the opportunity to do wrong. We also desire that all should refrain from sacrifices. If any should happen to perpetrate such a crime, let him be laid low by the avenging sword. We decree also that the property of those executed should be claimed for the treasury and that provincial governors be punished likewise if they neglect to visit penalties on such crimes. 1 December 356.

## Document 22: *Cod. Theod.* XVI.10.5. Constantius Augustus to Cerealis, Prefect of the City[24]

Let the nocturnal sacrifices allowed by the authority of Magnentius[25] be abolished and hereafter let such wicked licentiousness be destroyed. 23 November 353.

## Document 23: *Cod. Theod.* XVI.10.6. Constantius Augustus and Julian Caesar

We command that all those proved to be devoting themselves to sacrificing or worshipping images be subject to the penalty of death. 19 February 356.

## Document 24: *Cod. Theod.* IX.16.4. Constantius Augustus to the People

No one shall consult a soothsayer, astrologer or diviner. The perverse pronouncements of augurs and seers must fall silent. Chaldean wizards and others commonly called magicians because of the seriousness of their crimes shall not engage in any contrivance to this end. The universal curiosity about divination must be silent forever. Whosoever refuses obedience to this command shall suffer the penalty of death and be laid low by the avenging sword. 25 January 357.

24.  'Naeratius Cerealis 2', *PLRE* I, p. 197. In old age he proposed marriage to Marcella, one of the aristocratic women ascetic friends of St Jerome. She turned him down with the comment that what she wanted was 'a husband, not a legacy' (Jerome, *Letter* 127.2).
25.  'Fl. Magnus Magnentius', *PLRE* I, p. 532. He was a usurper from 350 to 353 before being defeated by Constantius II, and was married to the formidable and pious Justina who was later remarried to the emperor Valentinian I.

Document 25: *Cod. Theod.* IX.16.7. Valentinian and Valens Augusti to Secundus, Praetorian Prefect[26]

No one henceforth shall attempt during the hours of night to offer up ungodly prayers or indulge in magical preparations or funereal sacrifices. He who is detected in such and proved guilty we decree by our eternal authority shall be punished with a suitable penalty. 9 September 364.

Document 26: *Cod. Theod.* XVI.1.1. Valentinian and Valens Augusti to Symmachus (the elder), Prefect of the City[27]

If any judge, or official [*apparitor*] should appoint men of the Christian faith to guard the temples, let him know that he will be spared neither his life nor his fortune. 17 November 365.

Document 27: *Cod. Theod.* IX.16.8. Valentinian and Valens Augusti to Modestus, Praetorian Prefect[28]

Let the practices of the astrologers cease. If any be apprehended in public or private, by day or night, indulging in this forbidden superstition, both [he and his collaborator] shall suffer the penalty of death. For it is as blameworthy to learn forbidden things as to teach them. 12 December 370.

Document 28: *Cod. Theod.* IX.16.9. Valentinian, Valens and Gratian Augusti to the Senate

I adjudge that soothsaying bears no relationship to cases of magic, nor do I hold to be criminal this or any other religion practised by our ancestors. The laws promulgated by me at the beginning

---

26. 'Saturninius Secundus Salutius 3', *PLRE* I, pp. 814-17. A well-known pagan supporter of Julian who continued to hold office under the Christian emperors, Jovian and Valentinian.
27. 'Lucius Aurelius Avianus Symmachus Phosphorius 3', *PLRE* I, pp. 863-5. He was the father of the famous orator, held office under Constans and Julian and was Prefect of the City of Rome in 364-5 where he gained the reputation of 'a man worthy to be named among the outstanding examples of learning and self-restraint' (Ammianus XXVII.3.3-4).
28. 'Domitius Modestus 2', *PLRE* I, pp. 605-8. He was Prefect of the East from 369 to 377 and consul in 372.

of my reign bear witness to this; in them free opportunity was granted to anyone to worship whatever religion he had at heart. Nor do we condemn soothsaying, but we forbid it from being practised harmfully. 29 May 371.

---

## Document 29: *Cod. Theod.* XVI.10.7. Gratian, Valentinian and Theodosius Augusti to Florus, Praetorian Prefect[29]

If anyone, acting like some mad or sacrilegious person, should, by consulting the uncertain, involve himself in forbidden sacrifices by day or by night and should think that he may appropriate for himself or approach a shrine or temple for the performance of a crime of this kind, let him know that he will be subject to proscription, since by this just decree we give warning that God is to be worshipped by pure prayers and not profaned by abominable incantations. 21 December 381.

---

## Document 30: *Cod. Theod.* XVI.10.8. Gratian, Valentinian and Theodosius Augusti to Palladius, military governor (*dux*) of Osrhoene[30]

We decree by the authority of the public council that the temple in which images are said to have been set up, which may be judged by their artistic value more than by their divinity, and which was formerly dedicated for crowded assemblies and is also still in common use, should be left always open; and we do not allow any imperial ruling obtained by underhand methods to stand in the way. In order that the temple may be visible to the assembly of the city and be well-frequented, Your Experience must, at every celebration of votive festivities upholding the authority of our rescript, allow the temple to remain open but in such a way that no one believes that the performance of forbidden sacrifices is allowed because of the opportunity of access to the temple. 30 November 382.

---

## Document 31: *Cod. Theod.* XVI.10.9. The same Augusti to Cynegius, Praetorian Prefect[31]

No mortal man shall be so rash as to perform sacrifices in order

---

29. 'Florus 1', *PLRE* I, pp. 367-8. He was Master of the Offices (*Magister Officiorum*) in 380-1, under Theodosius, and Prefect of the East in 381-3.
30. 'Palladius 11', *PLRE* I, p. 660. Nothing further is known of him. The temple in question was probably at Edessa, the provincial capital.
31. 'Maternus Cynegius 3', *PLRE* I, pp. 235-6. He was an enthusiastic supporter

to obtain the hope of an empty promise by inspection of the liver and the forecast of the entrails or, what is worse, seek to know the future by an accursed consultation. The torture of a more harsh punishment shall hang over those who, in violation of our ban, attempt to discover the truth about the present or future. 25 May 385.

## Document 32: *Cod. Theod.* XVI.10.10. The same Augusti to Albinus, Prefect of the City[32]

Let no one pollute himself with sacrificial animals, let no one slaughter an innocent victim, let no one approach shrines, wander about the temples or look up to images created by the work of man, lest he should be found guilty under both divine and human law. Judges, too, shall be bound by this rule, that if any devote himself to a profane rite and enter a temple at any point whether on a journey or in the city with the purpose of offering worship, he shall be compelled immediately to pay a fine of fifteen pounds of gold and his staff also shall pay over the same sum with like haste, unless they have resisted the judge and informed against him without delay. Let consular governors pay six pounds and their staffs a like amount, provincial governors [*correctores* and *praesides*] four pounds, and their officials the same sum by equal lot. 24 February 391.

## Document 33: *Cod. Theod.* XVI.10.12. Theodosius, Arcadius and Honorius Augusti to Rufinus, Praetorian Prefect[33]

No person whatever, of any class or order of men of rank, whether he holds a position of power or enjoys an honour, whether powerful due to the lot of his birth or lowly by reason of parentage, station or fortune, in any place whatever or in any city should either slaughter an innocent victim to insensate images or with a more furtive pollution honour his household Lar* with fire, his Genius* with

---

of Theodosius and a fanatical hater of pagans. For the context of his activities: J. Matthews, *Western Aristocracies and Imperial Court A.D. 364-425*, Oxford 1975, pp. 110-11, 140-2.

32. 'Ceionius Rufius Albinus 15', *PLRE* I, pp. 37-8. He was a pagan and one of the most learned men of his time.

33. 'Flavius Rufinus 18', *PLRE* I, pp. 778-81. After holding office under Theodosius as Prefect of the East (392-5) he became the chief minister to Arcadius but was assassinated in the emperor's presence in 395. For details: Matthews, *Western Aristocracies*, pp. 134-6, 249-50 and Alan Cameron, *Claudian. Poetry and Propaganda at the Court of Honorius*, Oxford 1970, pp. 63-92.

wine, or his Penates* with incense; nor shall he light candles, or offer incense or hang up garlands.

1.  But if anyone has the audacity to offer up a victim for purpose of sacrifice or consult the quivering entrails, he may be informed upon by the accusation of anyone according to the procedure for high treason, and receive an appropriate sentence, even though he has made no plan against or inquiry about the welfare of the Emperors. For in the case of a serious crime it is enough to wish to pervert the laws of nature itself, to investigate illicit things, to uncover that which is hidden, to attempt forbidden practices, to enquire about the end of another person's life or to have hope promised from another's death.

2.  But if he should venerate images, formed by the work of men and doomed to suffer from the passage of time, by offering incense and should, by a ridiculous convention, in sudden fear of what he has made, either by garlanding trees with sacred ribbons or setting up an altar made of dug-out pieces of turf, thus try to pay honour to vain images with a gift which, though humble, yet is full of offence against religion, he shall be held guilty of sacrilege and shall be punished with the loss of that house or holding in which he is proved to have served a pagan superstition. For we decree that all places that have, for certain, given out the smoke of the fumes of incense shall revert to our treasury, provided, however, that they are clearly the legal property of the incense-burners.

3.  But anyone who should attempt the performance of such a sacrifice in public temples or shrines or in buildings or fields belonging to another — should it be proved the site was illegally used without the knowledge of the owner — let him be compelled to pay over twenty pounds of gold as a fine and let the same penalty for him who performs sacrifice apply to anyone who connives at this villainy.

4.  We desire that these provisions be upheld by the judges, protectors of the cities and councillors [curiales] of the individual cities in such a way that information gathered through them shall be reported to the courts promptly and the crimes so reported be punished through them. But if the latter group believe they may conceal or pass over anything through favouritism or negligence, they shall become subject to the wrath of the courts; if the judges, on the other hand, being duly advised of the infringement, yet delay punishment through connivance, they shall be punished with a fine of thirty pounds of gold and their staffs shall be liable to the same penalty. 8 November 392.

After the death of Theodosius in January 395, his sons, Arcadius in the East and Honorius in the West, continued his policy, with stern edicts against organized paganism and rural cults.

Document 34: *Cod. Theod.* XVI.10.14. Arcadius and Honorius Augusti to Caesarius, Praetorian Prefect[34]

Whatever privileges have been allowed under ancient law to priests, ministers, prefects and hierophants of the pagan cults, whether known by these or other names, are to be entirely abolished, nor should they pride themselves on being protected by any privilege, since their profession is known to be condemned by law. 7 December 396.

Document 35: *Cod. Theod.* XVI.10.15. The same Augusti to Macrobius, Vicar of Spain and Proclianus, Vicar of Five Provinces (southern and western Gaul)[35]

While we forbid sacrifice, we still wish the adornments of public works to be preserved. Let no persons who try to overthrow them beguile themselves with relying on any authority, assuming they can offer some rescript or law as an excuse. Such papers are to be torn out of their hands and returned to Our Wisdom. 29 January 399.

Document 36: *Cod. Theod.* XVI.10.16. The same Augusti to Eutychianus, Praetorian Prefect[36]

Let all temples in the countryside be demolished without disturbance or upheaval. With their overthrow and removal, all material basis for superstition will be destroyed. 10 July 399.

These laws in isolation provide a one-sided impression of a gradual erosion and abandonment of pagan practices. However, the constant reiteration of laws outlawing sacrifices and other cult practices demonstrates the limitations of this kind of legislation: pagan rites continued to be performed and tolerated. One such example in Rome was recorded for the year 359 by Ammianus Marcellinus

34. 'Fl. Caesarius 6', *PLRE* I, p. 171. A Christian who held early offices under Theodosius, he was the successor of Rufinus (n. 33 above) as Prefect of the East.
35. For Macrobius see 'Macrobius 1', *PLRE* II, p. 698, and for Proclianus see 'Proclianus 1', *PLRE* II, pp. 914-15.
36. 'Flavius Eutychianus 5', *PLRE* I, pp. 319-21. An Arian, he was Prefect of the East in 397-9, 399-400, 404-5 and consul in 398, and acquired the reputation of being a tough administrator.

and demonstrates the tenacity of pagan belief in times of crisis.

---

### Document 37: Ammianus, Res Gestae (History) XIX.10.1, 4

1.  ... meanwhile the eternal city was living in fear of an imminent corn shortage and Tertullus,[37] who was then Prefect [of the City] was plagued repeatedly by violent mobs, who were in a very menacing mood, entirely without grounds: for it was not his fault that the supplies failed to arrive in the ships at the proper time as the vessels had been driven into the nearest harbours by exceptionally high seas and contrary winds and were afraid of running for the Harbour of Augustus because of the great risk involved.

[2-3. Tertullus pacifies the mob by offering to surrender his little sons to them.]

4.  And soon after, by the will of the divine power which brought Rome up from infancy to greatness and pledged that she would last forever, just at the time when Tertullus was making a sacrifice in the temple of Castor and Pollux* at Ostia, the sea calmed, the wind shifted to blow gently from the south and the ships entered the harbour under full sail to fill the granaries once again to the brim with grain.

---

The effectiveness of all these laws, furthermore, depended on the stringency of their local enforcement. Occasionally, a prominent governor might be found using his influence with the emperor on behalf of a provincial cult, as was the case with Symmachus' friend Vettius Agorius Praetextatus, proconsul of Greece in 364.[38] This intervention is recorded by the historian Zosimus, a staunch pagan writing at the turn of the sixth century. It was a fundamental thesis of his *New History* that Constantine's acceptance of Christianity was responsible for all the empire's subsequent ills.[39]

---

37.  'Tertullus 2', *PLRE* I, pp. 882-3.
38.  'Vettius Agorius Praetextatus 1', *PLRE* I, pp. 722-4 and Documents 62-73. As proconsul of Greece he received a panegyric from the sophist Himerius and was honoured by the Greeks at Thespiae.
39.  On Zosimus: F. Paschoud, *Cinq Etudes sur Zosime*, Paris 1975; W. Goffart, 'Zosimus: The First Historian of Rome's Fall', *American Historical Review*, 76, 1971, pp. 412-41 as well as R. Ridley, 'Zosimus the Historian', *Byzantinische Zeitschrift*, 65, 1972, pp. 277-302. There is a complete English translation (*Zosimus, Historia Nova*, trans. J. Buchanan and H. Davis, San Antonio 1967), plus a not yet complete one, with useful commentary in French: F.

Document 38: Zosimus, *Historia Nova* (New History)
IV.3.2-3

(2) [Valentinian I] forbade the celebration of sacrifices at night[40] wishing by the passing of this law to prevent the celebration of the mysteries. (3) But when Praetextatus, proconsul of Greece, an outstandingly good man, said that this law would make life for the Greeks not worth living, since it would prevent the proper celebration of the most holy mysteries known to mankind, the Emperor repealed the law and gave instructions that the rites were to be celebrated in accordance with what had been ancestral custom from the beginning.

---

Paschoud, *Zosime: Histoire Nouvelle* (Budé) Paris, t.I (Books I and II) 1971; t.II.1 (Book III) and 2 (Book IV) 1979.
40.   *Cod. Theod.* IX.16.7 (9 September 364 = Document 25, p. 21).

# Chapter 2

# THE DEBATE ON
# THE ALTAR OF VICTORY, AD 384

For the Romans, *Victoria* was both a deity to be propitiated and a fact of history. She symbolized Rome's successful rise to power in the past and guaranteed the future greatness of the Empire.

In 29 BC Augustus set up a statue of Victory on a podium in his newly completed senate-house (*curia*).[1] The statue had been brought from Tarentum and was set up in the *curia* where it was adorned with the spoils of Augustus' victory over Egypt. Augustus also dedicated an altar of Victory which was placed near the statue.[2]

The statue itself does not survive but its form was probably the standard representation of the figure of a woman poised on bare feet with outstretched wings as if about to land, her long garments flowing behind her.[3] The Victory of Samothrace in the Louvre Museum and the statuette of the goddess in the National Archaeological Museum at Naples are examples of this type which is also found, in a simplified form, on the coinage of both pagan and Christian emperors.

The Altar of Victory was of major political significance. Senators traditionally burned incense and offered libations before the altar, on which oaths, including the customary oath of loyalty to an emperor on his accession, were also taken.[4] Such rites would naturally be offensive to the increasing number of Christians in the senate.[5]

---

1.  Dio Cassius LI.22.2. Dio was a senator and historian writing in the early third century.
2.  *Fasti Maffeani* (*CIL* I.1², p. 327). For detailed references: H. Pohlsander, 'Victory: the Story of a Statue', *Historia*, 18, 1969, p. 591.
3.  Compare Prudentius' literary description of Victory, written in the early fifth century (*Contra Symmachum* [Against Symmachus] II.23–38 = Document 49, p. 74).
4.  On incense and libations see Herodian V.5.7; on oaths see Ambrose, *Epistula* (Letter) XVII.9–10 ( = Document 39, pp. 32–3) and Symmachus, *Relatio* (State Paper) III.5 ( = Document 40, p. 36).
5.  It is not certain whether Christians formed a majority or not in the senate

On the occasion of his visit to Rome in late April 357, Constantius II ordered the removal of the altar, but not the statue, of Victory from the senate-house. Although he had expressed admiration publicly for the memorials of pagan Rome seen by him in the course of his visit,[6] his action was consistent with his recent legislation[7] forbidding the adoration of idols, the offering of sacrifices and the use of temples for pagan religious purposes as well as his donations of temple lands to favourites.[8] However, the altar was later unobtrusively restored, perhaps during the brief reign of Julian (361-3).[9] His successors, Jovian (363-4) and Valentinian I (364-75) allowed it to remain.

In 382, the emperor Gratian, under the influence of Ambrose, bishop of Milan (374-97), broke decisively with this policy of toleration. He confiscated the revenues for maintaining pagan sacrifices and ceremonies, diverted to the imperial treasury property willed by senators and Vestals to the upkeep of pagan ritual and abolished the exemption of pagan religious officials from compulsory public duties. This edict is referred to in a law of 415 stating that 'in accordance with the constitution of the divine emperor Gratian we ordain that all places assigned by the false doctrine of men of long ago to their rituals shall be joined to the property of our personal treasury'.[10] In the same year he ordered the removal of the Altar of Victory from the senate-house, but the statue remained. The removal of the altar gave rise to a flurry of diplomatic activity: a pagan deputation, headed by Symmachus, sent by the senate to protest to the emperor against the removal, was refused admittance. Meanwhile the Christian senators in Rome protested on their own account through Pope Damasus that they had not authorized Symmachus' embassy and would boycott the senate if

---

in 384. On this P. Brown, 'The Christianisation of the Roman Aristocracy', *Journal of Roman Studies*, 51, 1961, pp. 1-11, reprinted in *Religion and Society in the Age of St. Augustine*, London 1972, pp. 162-82.

6. Ammianus, *Res Gestae* (History) XVI.10.13-17 (= Document 2, pp. 3-4).
7. The relevant laws are Documents 19-24 (pp. 19-20).
8. Ammianus XXII.4.3.
9. The only evidence is Symmachus' statement (*Relatio* [State Paper] III.4 = Document 40, p. 36) that Constantius' removal 'did not stand for long' and the restoration is normally attributed to Julian, since we know that Julian ordered the restoration of pagan altars (Sozomen, *Historia Ecclesiastica* [Church History] V.5). It is odd, however, that a restoration of so important a symbol of the old religion should go unnoticed, especially in Julian's own writings. This probably indicates that the altar was, in fact, quietly restored after Constantius' departure from the city in 357, a view accepted by A. Piganiol, *L'empire chrétien*, 2nd edn, Paris 1972, p. 109 and J. Moreau, 'Constantius II', *Jahrbuch für Antike und Christentum*, 2, 1959, p. 169.
10. *Cod. Theod.* XVI.10.20.

the altar was restored. Soon after this, Gratian publicly renounced his pagan title of *Pontifex Maximus* which no emperor before him had done.[11]

In August 383 Gratian was overthrown and killed by Magnus Maximus who set up an independent court of his own in Trier (383-8). Gratian was succeeded in Italy by his brother, the thirteen-year-old Valentinian II. In the same year there was widespread famine.[12]

In July 384 Quintus Aurelius Symmachus took up office as Prefect of the City of Rome. His close friend and ally, Vettius Agorius Praetextatus, was Praetorian Prefect of Italy, Illyricum and Africa. The pagans' hand was strengthened by disunity among the emperor's immediate entourage in Milan, where Ambrose's position was threatened by the emperor's Arian mother, Justina. Symmachus took this opportunity to include among the state papers or *Relationes* — sent by him in his capacity as Urban Prefect to the Emperor — a petition for the restoration of the Altar of Victory.

In Letter XVII Ambrose has heard that a petition from Symmachus has been sent to the emperor but he is ignorant of its detailed argument. His immediate response, contained in this letter, is a statement of opposition in principle to whatever the pagans are about to propose.[13]

---

## Document 39: Ambrose, *Epistula* (Letter) XVII

Bishop Ambrose to the most blessed prince and most Christian emperor, Valentinian.

---

11. Zosimus IV.36. For the date: Alan Cameron, 'Gratian's Repudiation of the Pontifical Robe', *Journal of Roman Studies*, 58, 1968, pp. 96-9.
12. On the context of the famine and the conflicting evidence for it: J-R. Palanque, 'Famines à Rome à la fin du iv$^e$ siècle', *Revue des Etudes Anciennes*, 33, 1931, pp. 346-56.
13. Documents 39-41 are conveniently collected with a French translation by M. Lavarenne, *Prudence* (Budé), vol. III, Paris 1963, and with a German translation by J. Wytzes, *Der letzte Kampf des Heidentums*, Leiden 1977. The texts are re-edited, with a strong emphasis on technical points, by R. Klein, *Der Streit um den Victoriaaltar*, Darmstadt 1972, and discussed from a legal point of view by A. Dihle, 'Zum Streit um den Altar der Viktoria' in W. den Boer *et al.* (eds), *Romanitas et Christianitas*, Amsterdam 1973, pp. 81-97. Despite frequent discussion and the general awareness of its importance there is, as yet, no complete and satisfactory treatment of the topic in English but see A. Sheridan, 'The Altar of Victory, Paganism's Last Battle', *Antiquité Classique*, 35, 1966, pp. 186-206 and Pohlsander, 'Victory'.

1.  Just as all men under Roman rule serve you as emperor and lord of the world, so you, too, are a servant of the omnipotent God and his holy faith. For by no other way will salvation be assured except by each man offering sincere worship to the true God, that is the God of the Christians, who rules the whole earth; for he who is honoured in the depth of the soul, he alone is the true God: 'for the gods of the pagans are idols', as Scripture says.[14]

2.  So the man who serves this God and welcomes him for worship deep in his heart owes him not pretence or double-dealing but eager pursuit of the faith and of total devotion to him. If he cannot offer all this, he should at least not lend his countenance to the worship of idols or profane religious celebrations. For no one deceives the God to whom all secrets, even of the heart, are as an open book.

3.  Since, then, most Christian emperor, you should bear witness of your faith to the true God, along with enthusiasm for that faith, care and devotion, I am surprised that certain people have come to harbour expectations that by imperial edict you might restore to the pagans' gods their altars and also provide funds for the celebration of pagan sacrifices. These funds, which have for some time been vindicated to the public and private treasuries, you will appear rather to be donating from your own purse than restoring from theirs.

4.  They who never spared our blood, who overturned the very buildings of the Church from their foundations, complain about expenses. They ask too that you confer privileges on them, although they denied us the right of speaking and teaching, which is common to all, in the law of Julian not so long ago.[15] Those privileges were ones by which even Christians were often led astray; for they hoped to ensnare some by exploiting those privileges, some through their foolishness, some through the wish to avoid the trouble of expenditure on public needs; and because not everyone shows themselves to be brave, a substantial number lapsed, even under Christian emperors.

5.  Yet had these [privileges] not already been removed, I would have sanctioned their removal at your command. Although these rites have been curtailed and forbidden throughout the world by many previous emperors, at Rome, however, they were abolished and made things of the past by the rescripts of Your Merciful Highness' brother, Gratian of august memory, following the principle of true faith. I ask you not to destroy what your brother in his faith established, nor go back on your brother's precedent. In secular

---

14.  Psalm 95.5.
15.  The emperor Julian decreed in 362 that Christians should no longer be allowed to teach the pagan classics (*Cod. Theod.* XIII.3.5). Although the decree provoked some prominent resignations, it also aroused the disapproval of moderate pagans. Ammianus (XXII.10.7, cf. XXV.4.20) calls the law 'a harsh one to be buried in perpetual silence'.

business no one believes there is any need to fear that a decision once made may be reversed — yet is a principle of religion to be trampled underfoot?

6.   Do not let anyone cheat you because of your youth; if the man making this demand of you is a pagan, he should not entangle your mind in the chains of his superstition but rather he should instruct and advise you by his own zeal as to how you should pursue the true faith instead of defending empty vanities with such violations of truth. I, too, urge you to respect the high character of senators; but beyond doubt, God is to be put first, before all others.

7.   If advice needs to be taken on military matters, one should look for the opinion of a man experienced in fighting battles and support his judgement; when the question is one of religion, think of God. You injure no man in putting the Almighty before him. He has his own opinion to give. You do not force a man against his will to worship what he does not wish to; allow yourself the same right, Emperor, and let everyone put up with it with patience if he cannot extort from the emperor something which would pain him were the emperor to wish to exact it from him. The pagans themselves customarily dislike the use of double-standards; for every man should be free to faithfully perfect and preserve his personal belief and religious practice.

8.   So, if any calling themselves Christians believe such a decree should be passed, do not let their vacuous words convince you or their empty names persuade. He who urges this in effect performs sacrifice, as does he who decides on it; yet the performance of sacrifice by one man is preferable to the lapse of all. The whole Christian senate is imperilled in this.

9.   If today, Emperor, some pagan were to set up an altar with images (heaven forbid!) and were to force the Christians to assemble there to take part in sacrifices, to have the breath and mouths of the faithful choked with ash from the altar, dust from the sacrifice, smoke from the burning offering; if he were to give his opinion in that senate where they would be compelled to their opinion after swearing before the altar of that image — for they reason that the altar was set up there so that, as they suppose, each meeting of the senate should take place around it, although the senate now has a majority of Christians — the Christian forced to attend the senate faced with this choice would think he was being persecuted. This does happen sometimes, as they are compelled to meet for some wrong purpose. While you are emperor, then, shall Christians be forced to swear on that altar? What does the taking of an oath entail but the admission that he whose name you call to witness as the guarantor of your faith has a power divine? Is it in your reign that they seek and demand this course, that you should order the setting up of an altar and the granting of funds for pagan sacrifices?

10.   One cannot avoid sacrilege in the passing of this decree; therefore I request that you do not pass it, promulgate it, or lend

your name to any decrees of this kind. I, as priest of Christ, call
your faith to account. All we bishops would agree with this, if people
had not heard without warning the otherwise unbelievable tale that
some such measure was being put forward in your consistory or
requested by the senate. Yet far be it from the senate to be described
as asking such a thing; a few pagans are exploiting the name of the
whole assembly. For about two years ago at the time they were trying to put forward this request, the holy Damasus, Bishop of the
Roman Church, appointed by the will of God, sent me a document
drawn up by a numerous body of Christian senators, protesting that
they had not made any such demand, did not concur with the
pagans' petitions of this kind and did not give their consent to them.
They also complained, publicly and privately, that they would boycott meetings of the senate if such a resolution were to be passed.
Is it worthy of your times, Christian times that is, that Christian senators should be dishonoured so that pagans' unsanctified pleasure
should be put into effect? This document I forwarded to Your Clemency's brother [Gratian], whereby it was proved that it was not the
senate as a whole who charged its representatives with any mandate
about the financing of superstition.

    11. But someone may object, 'why did they not attend the sen-
ate while this resolution was under discussion?' My answer is that
they spoke their wishes clearly enough by not being present; their
words were clear enough when they spoke before the emperor. Yet
are we surprised that they rob individuals at Rome of the power
of resistance, seeing that they deny your freedom to refuse to swear
by what you do not approve or to hold by what you believe?

    12. Thus, with the memory of the embassy sent to me so re-
cently, I call again upon your faith, I call on your judgement that
you will not consider it advisable to reply favourably to a petition
of the pagans of this kind or add your subscription to such a reply,
in defiance of religion. At least bear in mind Theodosius the
emperor, father of Your Devotion, whose advice you have been in
the habit of taking on almost all the more important matters. Nothing
is more important than religion, nothing more elevated than faith.

    13. If this were a civil court case, the pleas of both parties would
be on record. The case concerns religion and I, as bishop, am the
advocate on one side. Let me be given a copy of the petition sent
you that I may reply at greater length. It was thus on all matters
that Your Clemency's father [Valentinian I], having taken advice,
would see fit to give his decision. It is certain that, should your decision be the reverse, we bishops cannot take it quietly or conceal
our resentment; you may come to the Church but you will not find
your bishop there, or you will find him obstructive.

    14. How will you reply to the bishop who says to you: 'the Church
does not ask you for gifts, for you adorn the pagans' temples with your
offerings? The altar of Christ spits at your presents, as you have set up an
altar to idols; the voice is yours, yours is the hand, the subscription is
yours and yours the deed. Our Lord Jesus refuses and spurns your

obedience, because you obey idols, for he said to you, "no man can
serve two masters".[16] Virgins consecrated to God do not have those
privileges of yours and shall the Vestal Virgins lay claim to them? Why
do you look for priests of God whom you have overridden in favour of
the unsanctified petition of the pagans? We cannot associate ourselves
with the falsehood of others.'

15. How will you reply to these words? That you were a child
and so went astray? All ages are alike perfect to Christ and all are
full to God. Faith knows no childhood; even little children, speaking
without fear, acknowledged Christ in face of the persecutors.

16.   How will you reply to your brother? Will he not address
you thus?: 'I did not believe myself conquered because I left you
to rule the empire; I did not grieve for my death because I had
you as my heir; I did not mourn my abandonment of rule because
I thought that this empire of mine, especially in the matter of holy
religion, would endure throughout all ages. Those triumphal inscriptions of a devout virtue I had set up, these profits won from the
conquest of earthly life, the spoils of the Devil, the plunder from
the enemy, all of which I offered, in these lay lasting victory. What
more could my enemy have done to me than this? You have cancelled my decrees, which up till now even my enemy who raised
his hand in arms against me had not done. The blow is the deeper,
for my laws have been condemned by my brother. My better side
is endangered by you; my death was that of the body, the death
you bring is that of my virtue. Now my imperial rule is cancelled
and, what is worse, it is cancelled by your acts and my kin, and
the merit obliterated is one which even my enemies applauded in
me. If you agree willingly, you have condemned my faith; if you
were forced to yield, you have betrayed your own. Therefore, the
crucial point, with you I am endangered.'

16a. Moreover, what reply will you give to your father [Valen-
tinian I] whose grief is the greater when he calls you to account:
'You have, my son, passed the worst judgement on me in believing
that I was prepared to collaborate with the pagans; no one informed
me there was an altar in that senate-house in Rome; never did I
believe so dreadful a thing, that pagans should offer sacrifice in that
assembly shared by pagans and Christians alike, in other words that
the pagans should insult the Christians present and Christians be
forced to take part in the sacrifice against their will. Many different
kinds of wrong-doing went on while I was Emperor and I punished
those who were found out; if anyone escaped notice at the time,
should he therefore be allowed to assert that I approved of him
because nobody informed me about him? You have judged me most
harshly if you think that the superstition of others and not my own
faith preserved my empire.'

17.   Therefore, Emperor, now that you perceive it would be an

16.  Matthew 6.24.

injustice, first to God, and then to your father and brother, should you pass any such decree, I request that you act in the manner you realize is conducive to your salvation before God.

The document to which Ambrose was objecting was Symmachus' third *relatio*, one of a series of forty-nine surviving state papers sent by Symmachus to Milan during his short term of office, dealing with many aspects of urban administration.[17] Although its power and eloquence moved many in the court who heard it read out, it must be viewed in the context of its time. The arguments used are conventional and are paralleled, for example, by Libanius of Antioch in his speech *Pro Templis* or by a pagan rhetor, Maximus of Madauros in Africa, in a letter to Augustine.[18] Moreover, many thinking people in Rome do not appear to have been affected by the debate which is not mentioned either by Augustine, at that time a protégé of Symmachus, or by Jerome, although both were in Rome in 384.

## Document 40: Symmachus, *Relatio* (State Paper) III

The Most Distinguished Symmachus, Prefect of the City, to our Lord Theodosius, forever Emperor.[19]

When first the noble senate, always your servant, learnt that wickedness was suppressed by your laws and saw the bad reputation of recent times made clean by our dutiful emperors, it used the authority of a precedent set in an age of prosperity in pouring out its long-hidden grievance and instructed me to be, once again, the representative for its complaints. I was then refused an audience with the divine emperor [Gratian] by certain unprincipled people because, Lord Emperor, right was about to prevail.

2. I am therefore charged with a double duty, to carry out public business as your Prefect and to put forward the case entrusted to me by my fellow-citizens as their delegate. There is no conflict of aims here, as men no longer expect their cause to be advanced by the support of courtiers, if there is disagreement on an issue. To be loved, admired, regarded with affection, these are greater

17. For details see the annotated translation of the *Relationes* by R. Barrow, *Prefect and Emperor: The Relationes of Symmachus A.D. 384*, Oxford 1973.
18. Libanius, *Oration* XXX.31ff.; Augustine, *Letter* XVI (Maximus' letter) and *Letter* XVII (Augustine's reply) — both translated in J. Baxter, *St. Augustine. Select Letters* (Loeb Classical Library), London 1930, repr. 1965.
19. Although the *relatio* is addressed to Theodosius in the chief manuscripts, it was most probably addressed to Valentinian II or to Valentinian, Theodosius and Arcadius all together. See Klein, *Der Streit um den Victoriaaltar*, p. 175.

blessings than ruling. Who could tolerate private feuds interfering with the interests of the state? The senate rightly condemns those who prefer their own power to the Emperor's reputation: our task is to keep watch on behalf of Your Clemency. More than any other cause the fair name of our age will benefit from the defence of our ancestral practices and the rights and destiny of our fatherland. That name is the fairer because you realize that you may not act in violation of the custom of your parents.

3.   We seek to have restored therefore the religious institutions that have served the state well for so long. One can of course list emperors of either belief and persuasion; the earlier practised the rites of their fathers, the later did not abolish them. If the religion of the former does not supply a precedent, let the impartiality of the most recent do so. Who is such a good friend of the barbarians that he does not want the altar of Victory back? We are cautious with regard to the future and avoid omens of change. If she cannot be honoured as a god, at least let her name be honoured. Your Eternities owe a great debt to Victory and will owe more still. Let those who have gained nothing from her turn their backs on her power, but do not yourselves forsake her friendship and patronage with the triumphs it brings. All men should pray to her power. No one, if he admits she is desirable, should deny her right to worship.

4.   Yet, were there no right way of avoiding this ill-omened act, at least the adornments of the senate-house should have been spared. Grant, I implore you, that what we inherited in our childhood we may in old age leave to our children. The love of tradition is a powerful thing. It was right that the act of the late emperor Constantius did not remain in force for long. You should avoid all precedents which you learn were quickly set aside. We concern ourselves with perpetuating your name and reputation so that future ages should find nothing that needs alteration.

5.   Where are we to swear loyalty to your laws and decrees? By what religious scruple will the mind of a deceiver be deterred from committing perjury? All is indeed full of the divine and the perjurer can find nowhere safe, but the most effective method of inspiring fear of doing wrong is the pressure brought to bear by the presence of the divine power. That altar binds the friendship of all, that altar guarantees the faith of individuals and nothing gives greater authority to our decisions than the fact that our order passes all its decrees as if acting under oath. Shall our seat of government, no longer holy, be exposed to perjurers? Will my glorious Emperors give their seal of approval to this act when they are protected by the general oath of loyalty?

6.   It will be said, however, that the divine emperor Constantius did the same. But let us seek to emulate that ruler's other actions rather than this one, for he would not have embarked on such a course had any other made such a mistake before him. The error of a predecessor may correct the man who comes after him and

criticism of the previous precedent provides the pattern for present improvement. It was right for Your Clemency's famous predecessor not to take precautions against unpopularity in an unprecedented situation; but surely we cannot claim the same excuse if we imitate an action we remember did not win approval at the time?

7.  So let Your Eternity follow the other deeds of that same emperor to a more worthy purpose. He stripped nothing from the privileges of the Vestal Virgins*, he filled the priesthoods with men of noble rank, he did not refuse expenditure for the ceremonies of Rome. Through all the streets of the Eternal City he passed, preceded by a joyful senate and viewed, with no anger on his face, the holy shrines; he read the names of the gods inscribed on the pediments; he inquired about the origins of the temples, expressed admiration for their founders and preserved these as part of the rites of the empire, even though he followed a different religion himself.

8.  Everyone has their own custom, their own ritual. The divine purpose assigned different cults to different cities to protect them. Just as souls are given to men at birth, so nations are allotted a genius* to preside over their destiny. There is also the question of services rendered, man's strongest argument for the existence of gods. For, as all reason moves in the dark over this, how can man gain greater recognition of the divine powers than from his recollection and factual proof of success? For if religions gain in authority from the passage of many years, we must keep faith with all the centuries we have known and follow in the footsteps of our fathers who followed their own with such good fortune.

9.  Let us now imagine that the figure of Rome stands before you and addresses you thus: 'Best of princes, father of your country, respect my length of years which pious observation of my ritual has ensured me. Let me employ the rites my ancestors used for they are not a matter of regret. Let me live my own way, since I am free. Through this worship I brought the whole world under the rule of my laws, these sacred objects drove Hannibal from our walls, the Gauls from the Capitol.[20] Have I been preserved then only to be reproached now for living so long?

10.  I will see what kind of reforms should be considered for implementation; yet correction of old age comes late and brings humiliation.'[21]

Therefore we ask that the gods of our fathers, our native gods,

20.  These are standard parallels from Republican history. The Gauls were driven off in 390 BC and ultimately defeated by Camillus (Livy V.35ff.), while Hannibal posed a direct threat to Rome in 211 BC, but was finally turned away by news of adversity elsewhere (Livy XXVI.8-11).

21.  For different applications of the idea of 'old age' in the period, see P. Brown, *Augustine of Hippo: A Biography*, London 1967, pp. 289-98. In the early fifth century Prudentius confronts Symmachus' 'old Rome' with a 'young Rome' (*Contra Symmachum* [Against Symmachus] II.649-65 = Document 49, pp. 75-6).

be left in peace. It is reasonable that all the different gods we
worship should be thought of as one. We see the same stars, share
the same sky, the same earth surrounds us: what does it matter what
scheme of thought a man uses in his search for the truth. Man cannot
come to so profound a mystery by one road alone. But such matters
are for men at leisure to debate; we offer you now not arguments
but prayers.

11. How much did it benefit your imperial treasury to revoke
the privileges granted to the Vestal Virgins? Is money allowed them
by even the most economical to be denied them by the most generous of emperors? Their sole distinction lies in their payment, as it
were, of chastity: just as their headbands lend glory to their head,
so their priesthood was honoured in their freedom from state dues.
They ask only the bare title of exemption, since they are safe from
any actual payment because of their poverty. Thus if they are deprived of anything it merely adds to their prestige; it is a truth that
virginity, consecrated to the public good, when lacking monetary
rewards deservedly grows in reputation.

12. Do not let the integrity of your treasury be undermined by
increases through savings such as these! Let good princes' revenues
be increased by spoils from an enemy not by confiscations from
the priesthood. Does that small gain compensate for the loss of
popularity? Greed is no part of your character. Therefore, those who
have been robbed of your support are in a yet more miserable state:
for under emperors who keep their hands off the property of others
because they resist the promptings of greed, the exactions made
redound only to the injury of the one who loses by it, as the power
that gains is not affected by the promptings of avarice.

13. The treasury even retains lands bequeathed to the Virgins
and priesthoods by the wishes of the dead. I beg you, priests of
Justice, that the right of accepting private bequests be restored to
the sacred institutions of your city. Let men dictate their wills secure
in the knowledge that what they have written will be honoured under
the rule of emperors who are free from the reproach of greed. Let
that happiness of the human race delight you. The precedent
afforded by this issue has begun to cause anxiety to the dying. Are
the religions of Rome, then, outside the bounds of Roman law? What
name will be given to this seizure of property which no law or crisis
has made uninheritable?

14. Freedmen receive legacies, and slaves are not denied the
proper provision made for their benefit in wills. Are only virgins and
priests of the sacred rites to be debarred from the security derived
from the right to inherit? What is the use of dedicating a holy order
to the public good and building up the everlasting empire with support from the heavenly powers, in adding their qualities to your
armies in friendly alliance, and to your eagles in offering prayers
for the good of all men, if you do not deal justly with all men? Thus,
is the slavery that hangs over men better than this? We cause harm
to the state, for it has never profited by being ungrateful.

15. No one should imagine it is only the cause of religion I uphold; all the set-backs experienced by the Roman people have arisen from actions like these. Our fathers' law bestowed honour on the Vestal Virgins and priests of the gods by providing enough to live on and the proper privileges; the endowment remained unaltered right up till the time of those small-time money-dealers who have diverted the funds saved for the upkeep of chastity to pay the wages of low freight-handlers.[22] Because of this deed a general famine has resulted and bad harvests have disappointed the expectations of all the provinces.

16. This is not due to infertility of the soil, we may not blame the winds, mould did not spoil the crops nor did weeds choke the grain; the year was scorched into barrenness by blasphemy. All were doomed to perish because religion was being denied its due. Let us blame the gravity of the famine on the changes of seasons only if there is some previous disaster as great as this one on record. The reason for this total barrenness is serious indeed. Forest twigs supported life and the peasants in their starvation flocked to the oaks of Dodona* for acorns.

17. Did the provinces have to put up with any such disaster when priests of religion were honoured by being fed at public expense? When were oak trees ever shaken to provide food for men in those days, when were plants pulled up by the roots, when did their joint produce supply by exchange the wants of other provinces, during that time when priests and holy virgins alike shared the distribution of corn? Sustaining the priests furthered the production of the regions and was a guarantee of profit rather than a free gift. Can there be any doubt that the funds were always given for the benefit of all, seeing that their removal has led to a general shortage?

18. It may be argued that the public funding was denied to a religion no longer that of the state. No good emperor should hold the view that something formerly granted from the public purse should be regarded as subject to the power of the treasury. Since the state consists of individuals, the money given out by her becomes again the private property of individuals. You rule over all but preserve each man's goods as his own and justice carries more weight

22. It was originally argued by L. Malunowicz, *De Ara Victoriae in curia Romana, quomodo certatum sit*, Diss., Wilno 1937, that the essential thrust of Symmachus' plea was not so much religious toleration as the restoration of lands and subsidies to priests and Vestal Virgins, and that he was thereby expressing the concern of the pagan aristocracy at having the basis of their wealth eroded away. This was accepted and expanded by J. McGeachy, *Q. Aurelius Symmachus and the Senatorial Aristocracy of the West*, Diss., Chicago 1942, and most forcefully by F. Paschoud, 'Réflexions sur l'idéal religieux de Symmaque', *Historia*, 14, 1965, pp. 215-35 (repeated in his *Roma Aeterna*, Rome–Bern 1967). There is simply no evidence, however, for the view that these lands formed a large part of an individual's total holdings (N. Baynes, review of McGeachy in *Journal of Roman Studies*, 36, 1946, p. 177).

with you than lawless self-will. Ask your own generosity for its opinion on whether what you surrender to others is still to be regarded as state property. Once surrendered to the discretion of the city, sums of money cease to be the property of the giver and through time and the growth of habit come to be expected, although originally a free gift.

19. If anyone should assert that you are making common cause with the upholders of the grant, unless you take upon yourself the unpopularity of abolishing it, he is trying to instil into your imperial mind a fear that is groundless. May Your Clemency have the support of the unseen guardians of all religions and especially those who helped your ancestors in time past. Let them protect you, while being worshipped by us. We request the religious establishment that preserved the empire for the father of Your Divinity, that made him a fortunate ruler and yourself his rightful heir.

20. That elder divine emperor [Valentinian I] looks down from his citadel in the stars at the priests' tears and blames himself for the violation of the practice which he himself was happy to retain. Grant to your divine brother and predecessor [Gratian] the reversal of a policy not his own: consign to obscurity an action by which, unknowingly, he offended the senate. For it is accepted that the embassy was barred from his presence so that he should not get to hear the public will. For the sake of the reputation of the past you should not hesitate to overturn a policy which was demonstrably not the emperor's will.

On the arrival at Milan of *Relatio* III, Ambrose, as he had requested, was given a copy. His Letter XVIII following is a detailed refutation of Symmachus' arguments point by point. As a result of Ambrose's intervention, the Altar of Victory was not restored and, with the death of Praetextatus late in 384 and Symmachus' resignation of the Urban Prefecture soon afterwards, the pagan viewpoint in the senate was silenced for some years.

Document 41: Ambrose, *Epistula* (Letter) XVIII

Bishop Ambrose to the most blessed prince and most merciful emperor, Valentinian Augustus.

1. The most distinguished Symmachus, Prefect of the City, has petitioned Your Clemency that the altar which was removed from the senate-house in the city of Rome should be restored to its place. You, emperor, although still in your earliest years, fresh in the flower of your youth but experienced in the worth of faith, must not support the petitions of the pagans. I offered a small treatise against this as soon as I found out, raising the points which seemed necessary

to the general drift, as far as I could understand it. Nevertheless, I demanded to be given a copy of the Prefect's petition.

2. Thus, while not doubting your faith but exercising the foresight of caution, although assured of your devout purpose, I reply to the argument of the Prefect's document with this work, asking only this: that you should make up your mind to expect not eloquence of language but the plain force of factual argument. For, as holy Scripture teaches us, the tongue of the wise man learned in letters is golden, it is armed with all the weaponry of speech, it flashes with the splendour of glorious eloquence like the sheen of the precious metal, it captures the eyes of the mind with its beautiful appearance and holds men fast by its look.[23] But if you test this gold carefully with your hand, it is valuable on the surface but beneath it is dross. I ask you to turn over and test with the hammer the pagans' sect. They ring with a sonorous grandeur, as if of value, but defend things devoid of the true gold of truth; they speak of God but worship an image.

3. In his petition as Prefect of the City, the distinguished senator puts forward three propositions where he thinks he has a good case: that Rome, as he says, needs to have back her own ancient cults; that payment should be offered to their priests and Vestal Virgins; that because you denied the priests their stipends a general famine followed.

4. On the first point, Rome wept for herself with a tearful complaint and she asked the return of her ceremonial cults, ancient, as she said. These holy objects, she argued, drove Hannibal from the walls and the Senones from the Capitol. Thus, while she asserted the power of the sacred objects, their real weakness was betrayed. For, by this, Hannibal had so effectively defied the sacred objects of Rome and her gods who fought against him that his conquering course had brought him right up to the city walls. How could men whose gods were fighting, armed, at their side have allowed themselves to be besieged at all?

5. As regards the Senones, what can I say? The Roman sacred relics would not have driven them off once they had penetrated the secret ways of the Capitol, if a goose had not betrayed them by squawking in a panic. See the kinds of guardians the temples of Rome possess! Where was Jupiter then? Was he speaking through the mouth of a goose?

6. Why should I deny that the sacred rites fought on the Romans' side? Yet Hannibal too worshipped the same gods. So they chose, then, the side they preferred? If the holy things on the Romans' side won, the Carthaginians were thereby overcome; if the Carthaginian rites triumphed, their gods could not then be any help to the Romans.

7. So let the Roman people hush that unhelpful complaint. Rome herself did not authorize it. She interrupts them with different

23. Proverbs 15.2.

words, 'Why do you stain me every day with the blood of innocent beasts? Trophies of victory are not to be found in the sinews of cattle but the strength of warriors. I conquered the world through a different discipline. Camillus went to war and brought back the standards taken from the Capitol, taking those who had vaunted their triumph on the Tarpeian rock; his military prowess overthrew men whom superstition had failed to dislodge. I need not mention Attilius [Regulus] who fought with death itself. [Scipio] Africanus won his triumph not among the altars of the Capitol but the battle-lines of Hannibal.[24]

'Why do you throw historical precedents at me? I hate the rites of Nero. Why mention the emperors of two months whose reigns ended almost as soon as they had begun? Or perhaps it has never happened before that barbarians left their own territories? Surely they were not Christians, those two who set a new, disastrous example, the one emperor a prisoner himself, the other making the world his prisoner, when omens promising victory deceived them and betrayed their own rites?[25] Perhaps there was no altar of Victory at that time either?

'Their failure makes them regretful: the grey hair of old age has brought a blush of shame to the cheek. I do not blush at Rome's conversion after a long life, along with the whole world. There can be no doubt that no age is too old for learning. Let the senate blush because it cannot mend its ways. It is the grey hairs, not of old age, but of good character which win praise. There is no reproach in improvement. The only thing I had in common with barbarians was that previously I did not know God.

'Your sacrifice is a rite of splashing yourselves with the blood of animals. Why do you look for the voice of God in dead cattle? Come, and learn the service of heaven on earth; we live here but serve there. Let God himself who established it teach me the secret of Heaven — not man who does not know even himself. Whom should I trust more on the subject of God than God himself? How can I have confidence in you pagans who admit you are ignorant of what you worship?'

8.    He says, 'Man cannot come to so profound a mystery by one road alone'. The object of your ignorance we know well from the voice of God. What you seek through vague hints, we have found through the real wisdom and truth of God. Your situation, therefore, bears no relation with ours. You beg from the emperor

24.  For Camillus see n. 20 above. The consul Regulus was taken prisoner by Carthage in 255 BC during the First Punic War, but refused to recommend peace in return for his life. Scipio Africanus won the battle of Zama against Carthage in 202 BC.

25.  The 'emperors of two months' may be the short-lived emperors of 69 (Galba, Otho, Vitellius) or 193 (Pertinax, Didius Julianus, Pescennius Niger) or of the period of anarchy from 235 to 284. The two emperors next mentioned are Valerian (253-60), who was defeated and captured by Shapur I of Persia, and his son Gallienus (260-8).

peace for your gods; we ask Christ for peace for the emperor himself. You worship the work of your hands; we regard it as offensive
that anything that can be made should be considered God. God
refuses to be worshipped in stones. Besides, your own philosophers
themselves laughed at those practices of yours.

9. You deny that Christ is God, because you do not accept
that he died – you deny that his death was of the flesh alone not
of his divinity, and by his death none, now, of those who believe
in him shall ever die. How unwise of you, to worship in an insulting
way and criticize with an honourable reproach! You think your God
is of wood – what abusive respect! And you believe Christ could
not die – what an honourable obstinacy!

10. He says that their old altars should be restored to the
images, and their ornaments to the shrines. Let them be demanded
by a partner in superstition. The Christian emperor has learned to
honour the altar of Christ alone. Why do they force the hands of
the God-fearing, the mouths of the faithful priests, to be associated
with their sacrilege? Let the voice of our emperor ring with Christ,
and let him speak only of the one he knows; for 'the king's heart
is in the hand of the Lord'.[26] Did any pagan emperor ever raise an
altar to Christ? While they demand back what previously existed,
they state an opinion on the basis of their own past actions on how
much Christian emperors should defer to respect for the religions
that they follow – seeing that then the pagans assigned all resources
to their own superstitions.

11. Our beginning was recent and already the gods they follow
are shut out. We boast of our blood, they are motivated by expense.
We see this as a victory, they regard it as an injury. Never did they
do us greater service than when they ordered Christians to be
flogged, proscribed and killed. Religious fervour made a reward out
of what they, in their delusion, thought was punishment. Look at
those noble souls. Through injury, through poverty, through punishment, we grew; the pagans have no confidence in the survival of
their rites without subsidies.

He says, 'let the Vestal Virgins keep their exemption'. This can
only be said by those incapable of believing in the power of chastity
without reward: let those who lack confidence in their virtue make
an issue out of money. Yet how many virgins have the promised
rewards created? Barely seven girls have been accepted as Vestals.
See the whole number attracted together by the sacred headbands,
the purple-dyed dresses, the processions on their litters surrounded
by their escort of priests, the enormous privileges, the huge salary
and, finally, the prescribed period of chastity.

12. Let them raise their vision, both of body and mind, and see
a populace of modesty, a nation of uprightness, a council of chastity.
Their heads are not adorned with headbands but with a veil poor
in its material but noble through purity. The allurements of beauty

26. Proverbs 21.1.

are not sought out by them but renounced. They have no ornaments of purple, no charming luxuries, but instead the practice of fasting: no privileges, no rewards of money. In short, all their way of life is such as you might imagine would, in the performance of its duties, deter from practising such a vocation. Yet, while their tasks are being carried out, their enthusiasm is strengthened. Purity increases by its own rewards. It is not a chastity purchased for a price but not preserved through any passion for virtue; it is not uprightness that can be sold off for money to the highest bidder. Purity's first victory is the conquest of the desire for worldly goods. Greed for money undermines the resistance of purity to temptation. Let us, nonetheless, lay down a generous sum to be doled out to virgins. What rewards can the Christians gain? What treasury is rich enough to supply such wealth? Or, if they feel the Vestals alone should be granted it, have they no shame that, although they claimed everything for themselves under pagan emperors, yet under Christian rulers these same do not believe we should have the same advantages as they?

13. They also complain that their own priests and sacred officials are not getting the public subsidies due to them. What a noisy protest erupted from them on this score! But we, on the other hand, were denied even the proceeds of inheritance from private individuals by recent laws, yet nobody complained;[27] we did not consider it an injury because we do not resent financial loss. If a priest sought the privilege of being exempt from curial duty, he would have to surrender the lands of his father and grandfather and all worldly possessions. How the pagans would exaggerate that grievance, if they had it, that a priest buys his regalia for the loss of his whole patrimony, purchasing his use of public indulgence for the sacrifice of all his comforts as an individual. While observing his vigils for the general good, he may console himself with the reward of his personal poverty, because he has not sold his office but stored up grace for himself.

14. Compare our positions. You are prepared to exempt the decurion, although you may not exempt the priest of the Church. Wills are drawn up to benefit the ministers of the temples, no irreligious man is debarred from the right to inherit, no one of the lowest condition, no one who squanders his reputation. The cleric alone of all men is shut out from the right all have and he alone, who joins with others in prayers for the public good, is denied the public right. No bequests are allowed, even from dignified widows, and no gift. Though no stain can be found on their character, yet they are penalized for their office and their right is denied them. The legacy left by a Christian widow to priests of the pagan temple is honoured; that left to the priests of God is not. I have included this point not by way of complaint but so that they should understand why I do not complain. I prefer that we should be poorer

---

27.   A reference to a law of Valentinian I issued in 370 (*Cod. Theod.* XVI.2.20).

in money than poorer in grace.

15. Yet they maintain that gifts and legacies to the Church were not interfered with. Let them tell us for themselves which temples had their endowments confiscated, as happened to the Christians. If that had been done to the pagans, it would have been inflicting injury by way of retaliation rather than an injustice. Is it only now that they cite justice in their defence and demand fair treatment? Where was that resoluteness of theirs when all Christians were robbed of their goods, when they grudged them the bare breath of life, when they denied the dead their due and put obstacles in the way of their achieving final burial. Those whom the pagans hurled into the sea, the sea restored. The victory of the faith is this, that the pagans themselves feed on the deeds of their ancestors whose actions they condemn. Yet, alas, is it not a strange principle, to request the payments granted to those whose deeds they reject?

16. No one, however, has refused the shrines their gifts, or the augurs their legacies. They are only being deprived of their estates because, although they defend them on grounds of religion, they do not make use of them in a religious fashion. They exploit the parallel with us, but why not the religious function as well? The Church possesses nothing of her own except the faith. This is its revenue, this its fruits. The property of the Church resides in the maintenance of the needy. Let the pagans list the prisoners ransomed by the temples, the sustenance they have offered to the poor, the exiles to whom they have supplied a means of livelihood. It is only their estates, therefore, that are taken from them, not their rights.

17. In retaliation for this action, so they say, there was a general famine to exact atonement for this piece of wickedness, because that which furthered the comfort of the priests alone had now begun to be used for the advantage of all. Because of this, so they say, the trees were stripped of their bark, which was torn off for food, and men faint with hunger licked at the miserable trickle of sap. Because of this they had to eat acorns instead of corn, were reduced to sharing the food of their cattle, supported themselves on a wretched diet, and allayed the torments of hunger in the woods by shaking the trees. These were, no doubt, events without parallel, which had never before occurred when the earth seethed with pagan superstition. Whenever before, in fact, did the crops mock the prayers of the greedy farmer with empty granaries or the grain ear sought for in the furrows disappoint the countryman's hopes?

18. And why did the Greeks think their oaks were oracles, unless they thought the provision of food in the woods was the gift of their heavenly religion? Such, they believed, were the rewards of their gods. Who but a nation of pagans ever worshipped oaks of Dodona*, when they would offer the poor fodder of their fields in honour of the groves? It is unlikely that the gods who were angry with them would have given as a punishment what they were in the habit of bestowing as a gift when appeased.

How is it fair that, in their anger because a few priests are denied maintenance, they themselves deny it to everybody, seeing that the punishment is much harsher than the crime? It is not an appropriate reason, therefore, which imposes such suffering on a failing world, so that the hope of the year while the corn is green suddenly perishes in its prime.

19. In fact it was many, many years ago that the rights of the temples were abolished all over the world; has it only now occurred to the pagans' gods to avenge their wrongs? If the Nile flood-waters fell short of their usual level, was this to avenge the losses of the priests of the city of Rome, although she did not so avenge her own?

20. But, given that they thought the wrongs of their gods were avenged last year, why do they make so light of them this year? The people of the countryside are not feeding on plants' roots now, nor looking for comfort from berries in the wood, nor pulling food off brambles. They rejoice in their prosperity, the harvests exceed expectation and satisfy hunger in full, giving an abundant answer to their prayers. The earth gives a full yield with interest besides.

21. Who so lacks experience of human life that he is surprised by the variations between years? But even last year we knew several provinces were overflowing with grain. Why mention Gaul which was richer than usual? They sold the surplus they did not keep in Pannonia; and Second Rhaetia found trouble resulting from her fertility, for a province safer in times of shortage roused the enemy against her because of her abundance; the produce of the autumn fed Liguria and Venetia. Therefore, last year was not made dry and barren by sacrilege, while this one has blossomed with the fruits of faith. Let them deny that the vineyards overflowed with the juice of their grapes. Thus our harvest with interest we reaped and profited also from an increased wine-harvest.

22. Finally, emperor, there remains the most important question of all, as to whether you should restore the subsidies that have helped your own position: for he says, 'let them protect you while being worshipped by us'. It is this, most faithful of emperors, that I cannot tolerate, that they make us liable to the reproach incurred by their prayer to their gods in your name, and commit a heinous impiety without your sanction, mistaking your tolerance for agreement. Let them keep their guardians for themselves. Let them protect their own followers, if they can. For, if they cannot help those by whom they are worshipped, how can they protect you who do them no honour at all?

23. 'But', he says, 'we must preserve the rites of our ancestors'. What of the fact that everything since then has progressed for the better? The world itself, which, in the beginning, saw the seeds of the elements drawn together through the void, to form a mass, while the world was young, and darkened by the chaotic terror of a work not yet complete — did not this world later with the separation of the sky, sea and earth receive the form by which it appears so fair

to us now? The earth, freeing itself from misty shadows, gazed in amazement on the new sun. The day does not reach full brightness at dawn but shines with increased brilliance as the hours pass, and the heat too increases as time goes on.

24. The moon itself which, in the prophets' oracles, prefigures the image of the Church, on first rising again to pass through her monthly cycle is concealed in darkness from our eyes. Gradually, her crescent waxes or she draws it out from the sun's domain and glows with her glorious clear light.

25. Previously, the earth was unfamiliar with the art of cultivation for food. Later, when the conscientious farmer began to assert control over the tilled fields and cover the uncultivated soil with vines, she was tamed and softened by cultivation and laid aside her overgrown aspect.

26. The first season of the year itself covers the plains with a uniform colour and is bare of growing things; but as it passes, spring makes her green with flowers doomed to fade, and finally mature with their fruits.

27. So we, too, in youth have the feelings of childhood; with the changing years we also change and lay aside the childish things of our unformed intellect.

28. Let them, therefore, say that everything should stay as it was in the beginning; they object that the world is freed from darkness because the glory of the sun has shone upon it. How much more welcome is it to dispel the darkness of the mind than of the body, for the ray of the faith to shine out than the ray of the sun? So the youth of the world, as of all things, has grown hesitant, so that the honourable old age of the faith, with its grey hair, may follow. Let those who object to this blame the harvest because its abundance comes late; let them criticize the grapes for ripening in the waning of the year; let them criticize the olive for coming last of all.

29. Our faith is a harvest too, a harvest of souls. The grace of the Church is the vintage of her services, which from the dawn of the world was green and flourished in holy men but in most recent times has spread among nations, so that all may understand that the faith of Christ did not insinuate itself into unsophisticated minds (for there can be no garland of victory without an enemy to overcome), but through the expulsion of the belief previously dominant, so that the truth might be preferred on valid grounds.

30. If the old rites gave so much pleasure, why did this same Rome turn to the rites of others? I do not mention the earth concealed under a precious covering, the shepherds' cottages shining with tarnished gold. To reply to the actual substance of their complaint, what of their reception of the images from captured cities, of conquered gods, rites of foreigners, setting up in rivalry of the sacred objects of superstition from outside? Where, therefore, did they get the precedent of mother Cybele* washing her chariot in a pretended river Almo? Where did they get their Phrygian prophets and the divinities of Carthage their enemy, always hostile to the

Romans? She whom the Africans worship as Celeste, the Persians as Mithras*, most worship as Venus*; the name varies but the divinity does not. Thus they believe even victory is a goddess, although she is something offered, not a power in her own right. She is a gift not a queen, she is the effectiveness of the legions not a power of reverence. Can this be a great goddess, then, who proves herself by a crowd of soldiers, or is granted from the outcome of battles?

31. They seek to set up an altar of this victory in the senate-house of the city of Rome, that is, where a substantial number of Christians meet. There are altars in all the temples, there is also an altar in the temple of the Victories. Because they get pleasure out of numbers, they perform their sacrifices all over the place. What is it but an insult to our faith to lay claim to the sacrifice of one altar? Can it be endured for a pagan to sacrifice in the presence of a Christian? Let them, he says, let them inhale the smoke through their eyes, even against their will, hear the sound of the music in their ears, feel the ash in their throats, the incense in their nostrils and let the ashes from our hearths scatter over their faces even though they turn their heads away. Is it not enough for him that his baths, his porticoes, his public squares are crowded with images? Is there to be no equality of status in that shared assembly? Shall the Christian part of the senate be choked with the cries of those calling their gods to witness, the pledges of men swearing such a faith? If he refuses to swear, he will appear to wish to lie; if he agrees, he associates himself with a sacrilege.

32. 'Where', he asks, 'shall we swear loyalty to your laws and utterances?' Shall your mind, therefore, which is bound up with the laws, receive its vote and accept the guarantee of loyalty with pagan ceremonies? Now the faith not only of those present but those absent and, what is more serious, your own, emperor, is under attack; for you compel them, if you so order it. Constantius of august memory, when not yet baptized into the sacred mystery, thought that he was polluted were he to set eyes on that altar.[28] He ordered its removal, he did not order its restoration. The former course has the weight of his action, the latter lacks that of his command.

33. Let no one soothe his conscience with the excuse that he is not there. The man whose spirit is compromised is more truly present than one who witnesses with his eyes alone. Mental bondage is more absolute than physical involvement. The Senate has you as its president to assemble a meeting and it meets at your order; it is to you it pledges its devotion, not the pagan gods. The Senators place you above their own children, though not above their faith. This is the love you should seek, this love, greater than empire, which preserves the empire so long as the faith is secure.

28. In accordance with contemporary practice, Constantius was only baptized shortly before his death in 361 (Socrates, *Historia Ecclesiastica* [Church History] II.47), so he was not a baptized Christian at the time of his visit to Rome in 357.

34. Yet someone may be swayed by the fact that a most devout emperor still lost all, as if rewards for a man's deserts were assessed on the chances of this world's events. Yet every wise man knows that the conduct of human affairs exists on a kind of revolving wheel. They do not always experience the same situation but change and alter for better or worse.

35. What man more blessed than Gnaeus Pompeius was ever sent out from the temples of Rome? Yet, after encircling the world with three triumphs, defeated in battle, exiled by war and banished from the bounds of his own empire, he met his end at the hand of an Egyptian eunuch.[29]

36. What king nobler than Cyrus of Persia was ever produced by the lands of the entire Orient? He, too, after conquering very powerful kings who opposed him and sparing the conquered, was routed and killed by the army of a woman. And that king, who had even given honours to those he had conquered, had his head cut off and put inside a bladder filled with blood to be mocked by a woman who ordered him to drink his fill.[30] Thus, in the turning course of his life, his deeds were not matched by their like but the reverse!

37. What man do we know of more devoted to the performance of sacrifice than Hamilcar, the general of the Carthaginians? He would offer sacrifice in his battle-line for the whole duration of the fight. When he learned that part of his army had been beaten, he threw himself into the very fires he had kindled himself, so that he might put out with his own body the flames which he now saw had been of no help to him.[31]

38. What, then, can I say of Julian? Through his excessive, ill-founded belief in the responses of soothsayers, he robbed himself of the means of return [from the Persian campaign].[32] Therefore, though disaster be common to all, the fault is not so shared. No one has ever been deceived by our promises.

39. I have replied to those who attack me as though I have not been attacked. My concern has been to refute the State Paper, not to expose their superstition. But, emperor, let the State Paper itself put you on your guard. For when he constructed an argument about previous emperors, he said the earlier ones of their number

29. The death of Pompey after his defeat by Caesar in 48 BC provided a moral for contemporaries.

30. The defeat and gruesome death of Cyrus the Great at the hands of Queen Tomyris of Scythia was recorded by Herodotus I.208-14.

31. While laying siege to the town of Himera in Sicily the Carthaginians were attacked by the forces of Gelo of Syracuse and in the ensuing confusion Hamilcar leapt into a sacrificial fire (Herodotus VII.166-7).

32. Ammianus, who followed Julian on the Persian campaign, claims that Julian entered the battle in which he died against the advice of his soothsayers (XXV.2.7-8) and in general was 'too devoted to prophecy from omens . . . a superstitious man rather than a genuine follower of sacred matters' (XXV.4.17).

worshipped with the ceremonies of their fathers and the later did
not abolish them; and even added that, if the religious practice of
the former did not form a precedent, the toleration of the more
recent should do so. In so arguing, he has clearly taught that your
duty to your faith is that you should not follow the precedent of
pagan ritual, and to your family that you should not contradict your
brother's decrees. For if they cited in support of their own argument
the tolerance of emperors who, although Christian, did very little
about abolishing pagans' decrees, how much more should you show
respect for the love of your brother in not abrogating his decrees,
since you should conceal disapproval even though you might happen not to approve? Thus you should now hold by the course which
in your judgement accords both with your faith and your relationship
with your brother.

A further deputation sent to Theodosius in Milan in 389 to request
the restoration of the Altar of Victory and the subsidies of the state
cult was again refused.[33] Two years later, in 391, Symmachus was
consul. In that year, Valentinian II was at Vienne and more liable
to be influenced by his pagan Master of the Soldiers, Arbogast,
than by the absent bishop of Milan. However, when approached
by the pagans, Valentinian again refused their request.[34]

Further approaches were made a year later to the usurper
Eugenius, who was backed by Arbogast, and, after initial reluc-
tance on Eugenius' part, the altar was restored, as was noted by
Paulinus, deacon of Milan, whose life of Ambrose was written in
422.

Document 42: Paulinus of Milan, *Vita Ambrosii* (Life of
Ambrose) 26[35]

But after Valentinian of sacred memory had met his end in
Vienne, a city in Gaul, Eugenius became emperor. Not long after
he began to rule, forgetful of his faith, he granted the request of

33. Ambrose, *Epistula* (Letter) LVII.4 (= Document 44, p. 56). This is probably
the occasion for the story, believed to be apocryphal, that the emperor was
so angered by the petitioners that Symmachus was whisked off in a carriage
and set down one hundred miles from Milan (Pseudo-Prosper, *De promis-
sionibus et praedictionibus dei* |On the Promises and Predictions of God|
III.38.2).
34. Ambrose, *Epistula* (Letter) LVII.5 (= Document 44, p. 56); *De obitu
Valentiniani* (On the Death of Valentinian) 52 (= Document 43, p. 53).
35. For details of Paulinus and the value of his work see the edition of the *Vita
Ambrosii* with translation and commentary by Sister M. Kaniecka (Catholic
University of America, Washington D.C. 1938).

Flavianus, at that time prefect, and Arbogast, the count, to restore the Altar of Victory and the funds for the ceremonies which Valentinian of sacred memory, although still a youth, had denied to the petitioners.

The triumph of Theodosius in September 394 must have been closely followed by the final removal of the altar.[36] However, the statue of Victory, which had never been removed, still remained: emperors were consistent in distinguishing between pagan shrines, which were to be destroyed, and works of art, which should be preserved.

The ultimate fate of the statue[37] of Victory is not known: possibly it was melted down during Alaric's siege of Rome in 410.

36. Claudian, *De consulatu Stilichonis* (On the Consulship of Stilicho) III.202-4 is often accepted as indicating that Stilicho restored the altar sometime before 400 (e.g. Pohlsander, 'Victory', p. 506 n. 1) but this is to misunderstand Claudian (see Alan Cameron, *Claudian. Poetry and Propaganda at the Court of Honorius*, Oxford 1970, pp. 237-9). Furthermore, the argument of D. Romano in *Carattere e significato del 'Contra Symmachum'* (Palermo 1955) that Symmachus headed another delegation in 402 which was attacked by Prudentius in his poem against Symmachus is now supported by T. D. Barnes, 'The Historical Setting of Prudentius' *contra Symmachum*', *American Journal of Philology*, 97, 1976, pp. 373-83. Given the highly literary character of Prudentius' work and its basis in the arguments of Symmachus and Ambrose in 384, the historicity of a 402 delegation is extremely doubtful (cf. Cameron, *Claudian. Poetry and Propaganda*, pp. 240-1).

37. This distinction between the altar and the statue is important, for scholars often confuse them. For example, Sheridan ('The Altar of Victory', p. 187 n. 13) assumes that Constantius II removed the statue as well as the altar.

# Chapter 3

# REACTION AND REVIVAL, AD 392-4

In 391 Theodosius, after defeating the usurper Maximus at Aquileia in 388, returned to the East leaving behind the young Valentinian II restored to his empire but under the guardianship of the Frankish general, Arbogast.[1] This control was much resented by Valentinian, who was finally found dead in mysterious and suspicious circumstances on 15 May 392, at Vienne in Gaul.[2]

The body of Valentinian II was brought from Vienne to Milan and placed in a porphyry sarcophagus beside that of Gratian. Over them both the bishop of Milan, Ambrose, delivered a speech in the form of a consolation to the two virgin sisters of Valentinian who were present in the audience. It was delivered in late July or August 392.

---

Document 43: Ambrose, *De obitu Valentiniani* (On the Death of Valentinian) 19-20, 52, 55

19. Rome had sent delegates to recover the rights of the

---

1. General accounts of these important years can be found in: A. Piganiol, *L'empire chrétien*, 2nd edn, Paris 1972; E. Stein, *Histoire du Bas-Empire*, 2nd edn, Paris 1959; J. Matthews, *Western Aristocracies and Imperial Court A.D. 364-425*, Oxford 1975.

2. For more detailed discussion of the contemporary evidence see B. Croke, 'Arbogast and the Death of Valentinian II', *Historia*, 25, 1976, pp. 235-44, who suggests suicide as the most likely possibility. On the other hand, F. Paschoud (*Zosime, Histoire Nouvelle* [Budé], t.II, 2, Paris 1979, pp. 455-8) discounts suicide on the grounds that, in his oration for the dead emperor, Ambrose places the unbaptized Valentinian in heaven (*De obitu Valentiniani* 51, 71-8). There is every possibility, however, that amid the conflicting reports at the time of this oration Ambrose was not convinced that Valentinian took his own life; while by 395 he was so convinced and therefore in his oration on the death of Theodosius (*De obitu Theodosii*) did not include Valentinian in heaven with his half-brother Gratian. In any case, it is odd that Ambrose should place in heaven a man who was unbaptized. Ambrose's special pleading (*de ob. Val.* 51-7) makes one sceptical.

temples, the unsanctified privileges of the priesthoods, and the worship of their own sacred objects and, what was worse, they were pushing their own case in the name of the whole senate. And when everyone present in the imperial retinue, Christian and pagan alike, was arguing that they should be restored he alone, like a Daniel, with the spirit of God awake in him, convicted the Christian advisers of falsehood and frustrated the pagans by saying, 'How can you believe that I should restore what my god-fearing brother [Gratian] did not take away[3] when it would harm both religion and my brother' — by whom he refused to be outdone in holiness.

20. And, when a parallel was drawn with the policy of his father [Valentinian I] in that no one had removed them while his father ruled he replied, 'You praise my father for not removing the altar. I did not do so either. What did my father restore to you to justify your demand that I ought to restore it? Even if my father had given it back at last, my brother had removed it! In this respect I would prefer to follow my brother. What? Was my father a ruling Augustus and my brother not? No, both are owed equal respect, and the services of both to the state were equal. I shall follow them both, so that I shall not restore what my father too could not restore, because no one had taken it away, and I shall preserve the state of affairs established by my brother. Let Rome, my mother, ask whatever else she desires; to my parent I owe affection, but even more do I owe obedience to the author of my salvation.'

[Later in the sermon Ambrose returns to the theme. The context of the following is the bishop's argument that, despite the fact that Valentinian died before being baptized, his virtuous conduct shall be rewarded.]

52. ... Grant, therefore, to your servant the gift of your grace which he never rejected, he who the day before his death refused the temples their privileges, despite the pressure from men whom he could well have feared. A crowd of pagans was in attendance, the senate was on its knees; yet he did not fear the displeasure of men so long as he found favour with you alone in Christ. How did he who had your spirit not receive your grace?

[Valentinian is now united with his brother, Gratian; the listeners would have been aware of the physical proximity of the tombs as Ambrose continued.]

55. Your father too is here, he who despised military service

---

3.   By asking that Valentinian restore what Gratian did *not* take away, it appears that this embassy (391) was asking not just for the restoration of the Altar of Victory and subsidies for the old religion, but for something more — perhaps the restoration of sacrifices recently outlawed (*Cod. Theod.* XVI.10.10 = Document 32).

and the distinctions of the tribunate under Julian through his love
of the faith. Give the son to his father, the brother to his brother,
for he imitated both, the one in faith, the other by equal qualities
of faith and devotion in refusing the temples their privileges. He
directed what his father had failed to do; he preserved his brother's
decisions intact. Yet still I accept the intercession for him to whose
reward I look forward!

On 22 August 392 Arbogast, after a few months spent in discreet
but unavailing overtures to the Eastern court, declared emperor
Eugenius, a former professor of grammar and rhetoric in Rome
and head of the palace secretariat at Vienne.[4] In 393, Eugenius,
as was common with new emperors, was consul in the West but
in the East Theodosius denied him recognition, appointing as his
own consular colleague the eastern Master of the Soldiery, Abun-
dantius. Previously the Western régime had included the Eastern
Augusti, Theodosius, Arcadius and Honorius, on the coinage but
this was now dropped and the administration of Eugenius went
on the offensive.[5] By the spring of 393 Eugenius had been recognized in Italy as well as Gaul.[6]

    The scanty evidence suggests that Arbogast and his puppet made
little effort to solicit the favour of the senatorial aristocracy in order
to expand the base of their support. Arbogast clearly relied on the
army and Eugenius had few contacts in the senate, although he
is mentioned in two successive letters of Symmachus to Richomer.[7]
Meanwhile, it was natural for Eugenius to do everything possible
to seek the support of bishop Ambrose. On being declared emperor
he wrote to Ambrose, perhaps in search of episcopal support for
his overtures to the Eastern court. The bishop did not reply, perhaps fearing that Eugenius would capitulate to pagan pressure for

4.    The best general accounts of the usurpation of Eugenius are J. Straub,
      'Eugenius', *Reallexicon für Antike und Christentum*, VI, 1966, cols. 860-78
      and, in English, Matthews, *Western Aristocracies*, pp. 238-58. Recent research
      has tended, correctly in our view, to stress the political rather than religious
      significance of Eugenius' régime (J. Szidat, 'Die Usurpation des Eugenius', *His-
      toria*, 28, 1979, pp. 487-508).
5.    For further details: J. Pearce, 'Eugenius and his Eastern Colleagues', *Numis-
      matic Chronicle*, n.s. 5, 17, 1937, p. 12 and G. Elmer, 'Eugenius: Eine
      historische-numismatische Studie', *Numismatische Zeitschrift*, 1936, p. 35.
6.    He is referred to in an inscription dated 14 April (*Inscriptiones Christianae
      Urbis Romae*, ed. de Rossi, I, 1449). Another inscription, from Capua, dated
      25 October must be put in 393 and cannot be used to show that Eugenius
      had already taken possession of Italy in 392 (O. Seeck, *Geschichte des Unter-
      gangs der antiken Welt* V, Stuttgart 1920, p. 538).
7.    Symmachus, *Epistula* (Letter) III.60, 61.

the restoration of the Altar of Victory and the temple subsidies.
In any case such an action soon followed.

At this point Ambrose left Milan, perhaps for Florence, in order
to avoid meeting Eugenius and Arbogast and from his self-imposed
exile wrote, in late summer 393, the following letter reminding
Eugenius of his duty to God.

---

### Document 44: Ambrose, *Epistula* (Letter) LVII[8]

Bishop Ambrose to the most merciful emperor Eugenius.

1. The reason for my withdrawal was fear of the Lord to whom,
as far as I can, I have been accustomed to direct all my actions
and never to turn my mind away from him or to place greater value
on the favour of any man than on that of Christ. I harm no one
if I put God before everything and, trusting in him, I am not afraid
to say to you, emperor, what I regard as my own opinion. So, just
as I have not been silent with other emperors, no more shall I hold
my peace with you, most merciful emperor. And, to preserve the
order of events, I will briefly review the happenings pertaining to
this affair.

2. The most eminent Symmachus, when Prefect of the City, sent
a State Paper to the younger Valentinian of august memory request-
ing that the property taken from the temples be restored. He carried
out his part in a manner befitting his own learning and religion. Likewise I also, as a bishop, had to acknowledge my part. I sent the
emperor two petitions in which I made clear that a Christian could
not restore the funds for sacrifices. I was not, I said, responsible
for their removal but I was responsible for the decree preventing
their restoration on the grounds that he would appear to be granting
funds for images, not restoring them. For he was not himself, as
it were, giving back what he had himself taken away but by his own
will he was lavishing funds on the expenses of a superstition. Finally
if he had done so, he either should not come to Church, or, if he
came, would either not find his bishop there at all or find the bishop
in the Church opposed to him; nor could he claim as an excuse
that he was a catechumen since even catechumens are not permitted
to provide money for idols.

3. My petitions were read in the consistory. Count Bauto,[9] most
eminent in the office of Master of the Soldiery, was present; also
Rumoridus,[10] of the same rank, an adherent of the pagan religion

---

8.  We use the edition of R. Klein, *Der Streit um den Victoriaaltar*, Darmstadt
    1972, pp. 161-71.
9.  Bauto was a Frank and Master of the Soldiery in the West from 380 to 385,
    consul in 395. See 'Flavius Bauto', *PLRE* I, p. 159.
10. Rumoridus was Master of the Soldiery in the West in 384. He became consul
    in 403, late in life. See 'Flavius Rumoridus', *PLRE* I, p. 786.

from his earliest childhood. At that time Valentinian heard my advice and did nothing except what the conduct of our faith demanded. His counts also agreed.

4. Afterwards I also raised the matter privately with the most merciful emperor Theodosius and I did not hesitate to speak to him to his face. When he heard of a senatorial embassy of this kind, although not the whole senate made this demand, he agreed with my notion. For some days I did not go to him, nor was he offended. It was because I was not acting in my own interest but because it benefited both him and my own soul that 'I was not ashamed to speak before the King'.[11]

5. A second senatorial embassy sent to the emperor Valentinian of august memory in Gaul was able to extort nothing. I was not actually there nor had I written anything to him at that time.

6. But when Your Clemency took over the helm of government it was learned subsequently that these concessions were made to men who, although outstanding in the state, were practising pagans. And perhaps it may be said, revered emperor, that you did not yourself grant them to the temples but gave them to men who had served you well. But you know that you must act with constancy in fear of God as is frequently done in the cause of liberty also, not only by priests but also by those who work for you or those included in the ranks of the provincials. When you became emperor the embassy asked that you restore the funds to the temples. You did not do it. Others asked a second time. You refused. And afterwards you considered the request should be granted to the same persons who petitioned you.

7. Although the imperial power is great, nonetheless consider, emperor, how great is the power of God. 'He sees the hearts of all',[12] 'he questions your conscience, he knows all things before they are done',[13] he knows the secrets of your heart. Do you allow yourself to be deceived and do you want to conceal anything from God? Did this not enter your mind? If they persevered so stubbornly it was surely your duty, emperor, in honour of the highest, true and living God to resist them even more stubbornly and to refuse what was harmful to the holy law.

8. Who begrudges you the right of giving others what you please? We do not scrutinize your generosity nor are we envious of the advantages of others, but are spokesmen for the faith. How will you offer your gifts to Christ? Few will take account of what you have done, everyone will take account of what you intend. Whatever they do will be considered yours; whatever they fail to do, theirs. You must, although emperor, all the more submit yourself to God. How will Christ's priests distribute your gifts?

9. There was a similar case in days gone by. Nevertheless, per-

11.   Psalm 118.46.
12.   Acts 1.24.
13.   Daniel 13.42.

secution itself gave way to the faith of our fathers and paganism disappeared. For when five-yearly games were being held in the city of Tyre and king Antiochus had come to watch, the most despicable Jason appointed some Antiochene spectators to bring 300 silver drachmas from Jerusalem and he assigned them as an offering to Hercules. Our fathers did not, however, give this money to the pagans but they sent some of their most faithful men and demanded that it not be paid for sacrifices, which was not appropriate, but given for other expenses. And it was proclaimed that, since he [Jason] said that the money should be sent as an offering to Hercules, it should be employed for the purpose for which it was sent. But because those who had brought it objected, in accordance with their own learning and religion, that the funds should not be devoted to a sacrifice but to other necessities, the money was handed over for the construction of ships. Although compelled to send the money they nevertheless set it aside not for sacrifices but for other state expenses.[14]

10. They succeeded in the end. They could have kept silent but it would have harmed their faith as they knew why the funds were brought. So they sent God-fearing men to make sure that the funds sent were allocated not to the temples but to the payment for ships. They entrusted the funds to the men who pleaded the causes of the holy law. Their success was the judge of their efforts which made their consciences clear. If men under the rule of a foreign power could take such precautions there can be no doubt, emperor, what you should have done. Just as nobody compelled you, no one held you in his power. You should have asked the advice of a bishop.

11. When I, at least, resisted at that time, although I alone resisted, yet I was not alone in desiring and encouraging it. Since therefore I am bound by my own words in the presence of God and all men, I have realized that I can do nothing else, nor should I, except to consult my own interest since I have been unable to retire from you unnoticed. I have for a long time, to be sure, repressed and hidden my grief. I thought no indication should be given to anyone. I must not now dissemble. I was not free to be silent. Hence I did not reply when you wrote to me at the very beginning of your reign because I foresaw this happening. Later, when I did not answer your request for a reply, I said 'The reason for this is that I consider that it will be extorted from him'.

12. Nonetheless, when an opportunity arose of performing my duty on behalf of those who were anxious about their position, I wrote and made a request in order to show that in the causes of God I have a proper fear and do not value flattery more than my own soul, and that I also display the deference due to your power in matters that should be asked of you, just as it is written 'Let honour be given where honour is due, tribute where tribute is due'.[15] For,

14.  II Maccabees 4.18-20.
15.  Romans 13.7.

> since I bow to private individuals from the depths of my heart, how
> should I not honour the emperor? But you who wish for deference
> to yourself, allow us to defer to him whom you wish to be recog-
> nized as the author of your empire.

The key figure under the usurping régime was Nicomachus
Flavianus who appears to have been the most influential and politi-
cally prominent man at the time. He was Praetorian Prefect of
Italy, Illyricum and Africa while his son was made Prefect of the
City of Rome by Eugenius and he himself became sole consul in
394. Nonetheless Nicomachus' spectacular involvement with
Eugenius and Arbogast appears isolated. His friends among the
Roman aristocracy, especially Symmachus, stood aloof from the
new régime.[16] In his letters from this time Symmachus' chief pre-
occupation is his son's quaestorian games, for which he indirectly
solicited Eugenius' support, thanking him with a gilt-edged invita-
tion to the games.[17]

The religious dimension of the usurpation displays the same narrowness. Under Eugenius there was no mass apostasy from Christianity and no widespread rejuvenation of pagan practices. While
Eugenius was nominally a Christian and used Christian motifs on
his coins he was probably religiously indifferent and therefore
offered no opposition to the industrious revival of Flavianus.[18]
Flavianus himself was an acknowledged expert in the art of augury
and in 394 consulted the Sibylline Books where he found an oracle
predicting the victory of Eugenius and the eclipse of Christianity
after a life-span of 365 years commencing in AD 29, the traditional
date for the death of Christ.[19] This oracle is best viewed as an
attempt to provide religious backing for the avowed purpose of
the régime.

By the last half of 393 some restoration of old shrines was being
undertaken. An inscription discovered at Ostia in 1938 shows the
Prefect of the Corn Supply dedicating a restored chapel to Her-

---

16. For Eugenius' relations with Symmachus, both before and after 392: B. Croke,
    'The Editing of Symmachus' Letters to Eugenius and Arbogast', *Latomus*, 35,
    1976, pp. 533-49.
17. *Epistula* (Letter) II.81.
18. For the activities of Flavianus at this time, exposing the isolation and narrow-
    ness of the 'last pagan revival', see J. O'Donnell, 'The Career of Virius
    Nicomachus Flavianus', *Phoenix*, 32, 1978, pp. 129-43.
19. Nicomachus as augur: Rufinus, *Historia Ecclesiastica* (Church History) XI.33
    (= Document 45, p. 60). The oracle: Augustine, *de civitate Dei* (City of God)
    XVIII.53.4. For the date of 394 : Straub, 'Eugenius', col. 870 and L. Herrman,
    'Claudius Antonius et la crise religieuse de 394 après J. C.', *Annuaire de
    l'Institut de philologie et d'histoire orientales et slaves*, 10, 1950, p. 330.

cules. It is headed by the names of the three emperors and states simply that 'The most distinguished Numerius Proiectus, Prefect of the Corn Supply, restored this chapel to Hercules'.[20] Under the later empire the Prefect of the Corn Supply was immediately subordinate to the City Prefect, who in 393-4 was the younger Flavianus. This restoration is, therefore, to be linked to the Flaviani.

The days of the pagan revival, however, were numbered. In the East, Theodosius had been assembling troops through the winter of 393-4, levying from as far away as Cyrenaica in North Africa, as a recently discovered papyrus demonstrates.[21] In the early spring of 394, Theodosius moved west with Roman troops commanded by Stilicho, Goths under Gainas and Armenians, Arabs and Medes. In the West, Arbogast collected a large force consisting mostly of Alemanni and Franks. On leaving Milan Flavianus and Arbogast proudly threatened that on their return they would stable their horses in the basilica at Milan and conscript the clergy into the army.[22] Meanwhile the army of Theodosius arrived on 5 September at the river Frigidus (modern Wippach) on the road from Sirmium to Aquileia.

In his continuation of the *Church History* of Eusebius, Rufinus (d.411) brought his account of the growth of the church down to his own day, ending with the triumph of Theodosius in 394. He provides most of the evidence for the pagan revival of 394 and he is an important contemporary source for the Frigidus battle which occurred not far from his native city.[23]

---

Document 45: Rufinus of Aquileia, *Historia Ecclesiastica* (Church History) XI.31-3

31. Meanwhile in the West, Valentinian, who ruled the state with a fervent spirit, as far as his youth allowed, strangled himself, for

---

20. This inscription was published and discussed by H. Bloch in 'A New Document of the Last Pagan Revival in the West, 393-394 A.D.', *Harvard Theological Review*, 38, 1945, pp. 199-244 and (with plates) in 'The Pagan Revival at the End of the Fourth Century' in A. Momigliano (ed.), *The Conflict between Paganism and Christianity in the Fourth Century*, Oxford 1963, pp. 193-218. For Numerius Proiectus see 'Numerius Proiectus', *PLRE* I, p. 750.
21. *P. Berl. Inv.* 13943 discussed by E. Wipszycka, 'Un papyrus d'Egypte et la guerre de Theodose le Grand contre la réaction paienne en Occident', *Eos*, 56, 1969, pp. 350-60. This papyrus is a receipt for payment of an extraordinary tax levied especially to provide for Theodosius' troops.
22. Paulinus of Milan, *Vita Ambrosii* (Life of Ambrose) 31.
23. On Rufinus: F. X. Murphy, *Rufinus of Aquileia*, Washington D.C. 1945.

reasons that are even now concealed from us. But some were sure that this came about through a plot of his general, Arbogast, and such was the strongly-held view of public opinion. Others said that the general had no part in the perpetrated crime but that there were reasons to do with him that forced the young man into this action, from resentment that Arbogast would not give him sufficiently unrestricted rule on the grounds of his strength being still immature because of his youth. There were, however, several priests, who had undertaken an embassy of reconciliation on the subsequent Emperor's instructions, who testified that Theodosius did not regard the general as guilty of the murder.

32. But he [Theodosius] was no less hastily spurred into vengeance, taking up arms against Eugenius, who had been set up in the place of the deceased [Valentinian], after having first asked the will of God through the agency of John the monk whom I mentioned before [in Chapter 19]. Then he [John], who had foretold that the first victory over Maximus would be bloodless, promised him [Theodosius] this victory too, although it would be attended by much bloodshed on both sides.

33. He therefore made preparations for war, seeking the aid less of arms and weapons than of fasting and prayers: he was protected not so much by the watchfulness of guards as by the spending of whole nights in prayer. Accompanied by priests and the populace [i.e. of Constantinople], he toured all the places of prayer and lay prostrate on his face before the shrines of the martyrs and apostles, and asked their help with devout prayers to the saints. But the pagans, who give new life to their errors by constant fresh misconceptions, renewed their sacrifices, stained Rome with the blood of their accursed victims, examined the entrails of cattle and, from the prophecies contained in the sinews, announced that Eugenius was sure of victory. Flavianus, then Prefect, performed these rites with heightened superstitious awe and with every strength of passion, and through his confident predictions — for his reputation as a man of wisdom was very high — they took it that Eugenius would certainly prevail. But when Theodosius, relying on the aid of the true religion, began to force the passes of the Alps, those demons to whom so many victims had been offered to no purpose, panicked, conscious of their fraudulence, and were the first to turn to flight. Their leaders and men learned in the pagan error followed them and, chief among them, Flavianus, more guilty through shame than through active wickedness; for, although being a learned man, he could still have escaped, he judged himself more justly deserving of death for his mistake [paganism] than for his crime.

But the rest drew up their forces in formation and, having stationed an ambush on the ridge above, themselves awaited battle on the mountain's lower slopes. Yet when the first came to engage, they promptly yielded themselves to their lawful Emperor, while the others who were caught deep in the valley fought with the greatest fury. For some time the victory hung in doubt: the ranks of the barbarian auxiliaries were broken and they turned to flee, but this did not happen with the purpose of causing Theodosius' defeat, but so that he should not appear to have won his victory through barbarians. Then, on seeing his forces routed, he [Theodosius] stood on a prominent rock where he could see and be seen by both armies, hurled away his weapons and turned to aid he could trust, casting himself down in the sight of God. 'Almighty God', he said, 'you know that I entered on this war of just retribution, as I think, in the name of Christ your son; if it be otherwise, punish me now. But if I came to this place with a righteous cause, trusting in you, stretch out your right hand to your own people, lest the pagans chance to say, "Where is their God?" ' In their certainty that their pious Emperor's prayer had been heard by God, the generals present gained heart for the slaughter. Prominent among them was Bacurius, a man distinguished for his faith, holiness, manliness and good qualities of body and mind, the type of man who deserved to be a companion and associate of Theodosius. He wrought widespread havoc among the enemy closest to him with his spear, javelins and sword and broke through the ranks of the enemy, crowded and close-packed though they were. He pushed through thousands of fugitives to the usurper himself, shattering their columns and spreading destruction far and wide. It may perhaps be hard for the pagans to believe what happened; for it was discovered that, after the prayer that the Emperor poured out to God, such a fierce wind arose as to turn the weapons of the enemy back on those who hurled them. When the wind persisted with great force and every missile launched by the enemy was foiled, their spirit gave way, or rather it was shattered by the divine power. Despite the brave behaviour of Arbogast, which was in vain because God opposed him, Eugenius was brought to the feet of Theodosius, his hands tied behind his back, and that was the end of both his life and his struggle.

Then indeed did that victory prove more glorious to the devout Emperor through the defeat of the pagans' views than it did through the death of the usurper: for their empty hope and false divination brought less punishment to those that died than it perpetuated shame to those that survived.[24]

Knowing how slight was the support for Eugenius and Arbogast, Theodosius could afford to show mercy in victory. Even the closest supporters of the régime, with the exception of Arbogast, Eugenius and the elder Flavianus himself, were spared. The younger Flavianus, the Prefect of the City, had his estates restored and Marcianus, appointed proconsul of Africa, was forgiven after Ambrose,

24. For the Frigidus battle see O. Seeck and G. Veith, 'Die Schlacht am Frigidus', *Klio*, 13, 1913, pp. 451-67 and Paschoud, *Zosime. Histoire Nouvelle*, pp. 474-500 (in conjunction with the excellent map at the back of the volume).

at Symmachus' request, had interceded on his behalf.[25] Several laws, while annulling some acts of the usurper, granted pardons to Eugenius' supporters in the civil service and upheld military discharges obtained in his time. The period of the usurpation, it was decreed, should be thought of 'as if it had not been'.[26] Theodosius' clemency was praised by contemporaries and later writers alike.

After the battle Theodosius moved into Italy, probably to Rome itself. At least Zosimus, following the unreliable Eunapius, records a visit of Theodosius to Rome late in 394. Its existence is controversial, but the action of Theodosius in abolishing sacrifices and pagan senatorial resistance to it has some elements of truth, as the Christian emperor's first duty was clearly to annul the pro-pagan measures of Eugenius.[27]

---

Document 46: Zosimus, *Historia Nova* (New History) IV.59.1-3

1. After his success thus far, Theodosius visited Rome and there proclaimed Augustus[28] his son Honorius, while at the same time creating Stilicho Master of the Soldiers there and leaving him behind as guardian of his son. Having summoned the Senate, which still abided by its ancient rites handed down from our ancestors and which was not to be brought to agree with those who despised the gods, he addressed it, exhorting it to abandon what he called its previously held 'error' and take up the Christian faith, the message of which is forgiveness for every sin and every impiety.

2. Nobody obeyed his call nor was anyone persuaded either to abandon the ancestral rites transmitted to them from the foundation of the city or to prefer to them an absurd belief (for by constant adherence to their former rites for about one thousand two hundred years their city had remained unconquered, whereas they were ignorant of the consequences if they exchanged this faith for another). Theodosius therefore at this point announced that the expense of pagan rites and sacrifices was a burden on the public

---

25.   Symmachus, *Epistula* (Letter) III.33 (= Document 90, p. 119).
26.   *Cod. Theod.* XV.14.9.
27.   The case against the historicity of the visit to Rome in 394 is set out by W. Ensslin, 'War Kaiser Theodosius I zweimal in Rom?', *Hermes*, 81, 1953, pp. 500-7 and F. Paschoud, *Cinq Etudes sur Zosime*, Paris 1975, pp. 100-83; the case for by Alan Cameron, 'Theodosius the Great and the Regency of Stilico', *Harvard Studies in Classical Philology*, 73, 1969, pp. 248-64.
28.   Incorrect. Honorius was actually proclaimed *Augustus* at the Hebdomon, near Constantinople, on 23 January 393 ('Fl. Honorius 3', *PLRE* I, p. 442).

treasury and that he intended to abolish them, as he did not approve of their performance and, moreover, that further funds were required for military expenditure.

3.  The senators in their turn declared that the rites could not properly be performed except at public expense. Yet, with the abolition of sacrifices by law and the neglect of other rites handed down from our fathers, the Roman Empire gradually declined and became the home of barbarians . . .

Theodosius' treatment of the Roman Senate is also outlined in the first book of Prudentius' poem *Against Symmachus*, an attack on all aspects of paganism (lines 42-407) framed by extensive panegyric of Theodosius, his victory over usurpation, and his 'conversion' of the Senate to Christianity. The context is clearly that of late 394.

However, the poem as a whole was completed in the spring of 402 and may coincide with a pilgrimage to Rome by the poet. By its title, it purports to continue the debate on the Altar of Victory of 384, and may have been inspired by the letters of Ambrose, although the date of their publication is not certain. Alternatively the poem may have been prompted by the death of Symmachus which is assumed, from the abrupt cessation of his correspondence after his journey to Milan of February 402, to have taken place early that year, or by the publication of Symmachus' own works.[29]

Document 47: Prudentius, *Contra Symmachum* (Against Symmachus) I.1-41, 408-16, 442-642

Preface (lines 1-41)

I once thought that the city [of Rome], sick with her pagan faults, had already shaken off the dangers of her ancient disease and no evil remained, now that the Emperor's healing care had allayed the

29.  On the publication of Ambrose's letters which also contained Symmachus' third *Relatio*: R. Klein, 'Die Kaiserbriefe des Ambrosius. Zur Problematik ihrer Veröffentlichung', *Athenaeum*, n.s. 14, 1970, pp. 335-71. All that is known of Symmachus' letters is that they were published by his son after his father's death. There is no reason to believe they were not published immediately. On the other hand, it has been suggested (most recently by T. D. Barnes, 'The Historical Setting of Prudentius' *contra Symmachum*', *American Journal of Philology*, 97, 1976, pp. 373-86) that Prudentius' poem was designed to counteract another petition of Symmachus to the imperial court at Milan in 402. Such a delegation is, however, unlikely (see above, p. 51 n. 36).

excessive troubles in the citadel. (5) Yet, since the revived plague now aims to assault the safety of the people of Romulus, we must beg our father for a cure. Let him not allow Rome to be defiled by her ancient vileness, nor the togas of her leading men to be stained with smoke and blood. Did that glorious father of his country and controller of the world (10) achieve nothing therefore by outlawing the former error which considered as gods shapes that wandered beneath the dark ether or sanctified in place of the supreme godhead the natural elements, which are the creation of the Father who created all? It was the concern of this man only that the wound in the country's soul (15) should not display merely a surface scar on the skin, while the superficial closing nursed, hidden deep inside, a festering wound, eaten away with putrefaction because of the surgeon's deceit. But he was keen that the nobler part of the man within should live (20) and understand how to preserve his soul, already purified of the fatal disease, safe from the internal poison. The cure offered by the usurpers before him had been to see what would suit the immediate and temporary situation confronting them, and take no thought for the future. (25) Wickedly, alas, did they serve their people, wickedly did they flatter the Senators themselves whom they allowed to be thrown headlong into hell along with Jupiter* and the great crowd of gods! But this Emperor extends his rule beyond the present by desiring to establish the salvation of his people. (30) Attractive indeed is the statement of a certain wise man: 'a state would be fortunate enough were her kings wise, or her wise men kings'.[30] Is not this Emperor one of the few who, having gained the throne, still cultivated the teaching of divine wisdom? (35) Behold, in him mankind and the toga-clad race have found a leader who is also wise. With justice on the throne our fortunate Roman state thrives. Obey a teacher who is also your ruler. He warns you that the most base error and superstition of your ancestors must depart, (40) nor must you suppose that there is any god but he who is supreme above all and who created the immeasurable space of the great world.

## Theodosius' address to Rome (lines 408-16, 442-505)

These then were the rites derived from our earliest ancestors which entangled and corrupted the imperial court (410) when our Emperor, twice victorious after the deaths of two usurpers, fixed his triumphal gaze on her handsome walls. He beheld a city surrounded by black clouds; in the dark obscurity of night the polluted air shut out the calm black sky from the city of the seven hills. (415) He groaned in pity for her and spoke as follows:

'Loyal mother, lay aside your garments of sorrow (416-42) ... Let not your god be earth, nor your god be a star in the sky, nor the ocean, nor a force hidden beneath the earth, condemned to

30.  Plato, *Republic* V.473d.

infernal darkness because of its accursed deeds. (445) Do not make
a god of the virtues of men, nor the wandering and insubstantial
shapes of souls or spirits. Do not let a ghost be a god to you, or
a guardian spirit, or a location, or a phantom that flies through the
winds of the air. Let these pagan divinities belong only to rustic barbarians. (450) Among them everything is sacred that fear has persuaded them to hold in awe: signs and prodigies compel them to
believe in dreadful gods who delight in their habit of devouring
blood, so that a fattened victim is torn to pieces in a deep grove
for its flesh to be devoured, washed down by draughts of wine.
(455) It is unbecoming and pathetic that you, after giving law and
justice to conquered tribes and teaching throughout the world those
whose warfare and customs were savage to know gentleness,
should, in clinging to superstition, hold the same views as primitive
peoples do in their savage ways (460) and unreasonably follow in
their ignorance. Whether battle awaits us, or whether we may lay
down laws in undisturbed peace, or whether we trample on the
necks of two conquered usurpers in the city's heart, you, Royal City,
must freely acknowledge my standards, (465) on which the sign of
the Cross is carried before me, shining bejewelled or fastened in
solid gold on the long spear-shafts. By this sign did the invincible
avenger Constantine cross the Alps and release you from that miserable servitude you experienced when Maxentius oppressed you with
his pernicious court.[31] (470) You were mourning, as you yourself
know, a hundred senators condemned to a long captivity. If a bride-
groom bemoaned the breaking of the marriage settlement, his promised bride stolen by some accursed accomplice, he was plunged
into a dark dungeon in cruel chains to atone; or if a bride was
ordered to ascend to the royal bed (475) and had begun to please
the master's polluted lust, her husband's indignation resulted in
death. The ferocious prince's prisons were full of the fathers of young
girls. If a parent murmured his complaints at his daughter's abduction
too bitterly, the betrayal of his resentment or sighs which gave away
too much (480) were not allowed to pass unpunished. The Milvian
bridge bore witness to the Christian general's approach to the city
when it hurled the usurper headlong into the waters of the Tiber,
testifying to the nature of the power it saw directing the victorious
army, the standard the avenging hand (485) carried in the vanguard,
the sign that gleamed on the spears. Christ was the symbol that
marked the purple labarum, woven in golden jewels, Christ had
traced the devices on the shields, and on the helmet crests the Cross
blazed out. The most distinguished order of senators recalls that day
(490) when it came out with matted hair, filthy, loaded with prison-
chains or bound with heavy fetters and, clasping the victor's feet,

---

31.  The day before the battle against Maxentius (28 October 312) Constantine
     saw in the sky the sign of the Cross which he took as portending the favour
     of the Christian God. He subsequently had a spear fashioned into a splendid
     cross-shape to serve as the standard for his army (Eusebius, *Life of Constantine*
     I.28-31).

fell prostrate in tears before the glorious banners. On that day did the senate worship the device carried by the avenging army, (495) the honoured name of Christ which shone upon its weapons. Take heed, therefore, illustrious capital of the world, that you do not hereafter invent prodigies without substance and ghosts with their stinking ceremonial and reject the power of the true God, which you have experienced. Please now lay aside your childish festivals, (500) your absurd rites and your offerings unworthy of so great an empire. Wash clean, O nobles, the marbles, sprinkled and stained as they are with rotten blood; let the statues, works of great sculptors, stand clean; let these become the fairest adornments of our city, (505) and grant that these works of art be not discoloured by misuse or perverted to a sinful purpose.'

## The conversion of Rome (lines 506-43)

By edicts such as these was the City educated to abandon her old errors and shook the dark clouds from her wrinkled face. The nobles were now ready to try the paths of eternity and, at their greatsouled leader's bidding, to follow Christ (510) and place their hopes in everlasting life. Then, in her old age, for the first time Rome, keen to learn, blushed at her own history; now is she ashamed of time past and hates the years gone by together with their religious ceremonies. As soon as she, recalling how the fields bordering the ditches of her walls (515) had been soaked with just men's innocent blood, sees around her a thousand reproachful tombs, still more deeply does she repent her cruel judgement, her uncontrolled assertion of power, her over-violent anger in the cause of a shameful religion. She desires to compensate for the dreadful wounds inflicted through injuring (520) justice by offering obedience, though late, and asking forgiveness. In order to absolve her great empire of the charge of cruelty in her past rejection of holiness she searches after the atonement indicated to her and converts to faith in Christ with total devotion. The laurels of the victorious Marius when he dragged the Numidian Jugurtha[32] behind him in triumph to the people's applause were less beneficial to the city (525) than this. Nor with the execution of Cethegus, justly thrown into prison,[33] did the consul from Arpinum [Cicero] bring you, Rome, so great a cure for disease as the benefit our emperor in our own time has perceived and granted to you. Many a Catiline (530) did he [Theodosius] cast out, who was plotting, not raging fires for our houses or assassinations for our senators, but the blackness of Hell for our soul and torments for the inner life of men. Enemies wandered everywhere through the temples and courtyards: they held sway in the forum and the

32.  Marius celebrated his defeat of the Numidian king, Jugurtha, in Rome in 104 BC.

33.  Cethegus was one of the senators involved with Catiline in his conspiracy in 63 BC when Cicero was consul and responsible for uncovering the conspiracy and punishing the offenders.

high Capitol; (535) while they plotted treacherous attacks on the very hearts of the people, they had made a practice of instilling the plague silently into their marrow, by means of the serpent's poison. Thus he triumphs in peace over his stealthy foe, bringing home glorious trophies of victory without bloodshed, and he teaches the State of Quirinus [Rome] (540) to reign forever over a heavenly kingdom. No bounds, in truth, has he set, he places no limits in time: he teaches them to hold power without end that the Romulean [Roman] virtue might never grow old, nor the glory she has procured know old age.

## The Christian Senate (lines 544-77)

You may see the Senators, the most glorious lights of the world, rejoice, (545) that council of old Catos eager to wear a whiter toga, the snow-white garment of holiness, and lay aside their pontifical vestments. Only a few are left on the Tarpeian Rock as Evander's[34] senate, the descendants of the house of Amnius, the glorious off-spring of the Probi, (550) now hasten to the pure sanctuaries of the Nazarenes, the [baptismal] fonts of the apostles.[35] For it is said that a high-born Anicius was foremost in shedding glory on the city's head, as is proud Rome's own boast.[36] The heir of the blood and name of Olybrius, too, (555) though entered in the lists of consuls and distinguished by the palm-decorated coat, eagerly lowered the rods of Brutus before a martyr's doors and made the Ausonian [Italian] axe bow to Christ.[37] The ready faith of a Paulinus or a Bassus did not hesitate to dedicate itself to Christ and raise the head of a proud, patrician line (560) to meet the era to come.[38] Why should I review in this poem the Gracchi, the friends of the people, supported by the right of official power, eminent among the highest in the senate, who ordered images of the gods to be pulled down and, with their lictors, offered themselves (565) humbly to Christ the Almighty to be ruled by him?[39] One may count hundreds of ancient noble houses who have turned to the banner of Christ and raised themselves from the vast depths of shameful idolatry. If the city has any identity or any standing it lies in these men; (570) if the more

---

34. Evander was a mythical Greek king who settled on the site of Rome.
35. The Annii and the Probi were among the most distinguished Roman senatorial families. For the process of Christianization: P. Brown, 'The Christianisation of the Roman Aristocracy', *Journal of Roman Studies* 51, 1961, pp. 1-11 (reprinted in *Religion and Society in the Age of Saint Augustine*, London 1972, pp. 161-82).
36. Presumably a reference to the consul of 371, Sextus Claudius Petronius Probus (see Documents 81-6, pp. 115-18).
37. The consul of 379 'Q. Clodius Hermogenianus Olybrius 3', *PLRE* I, p. 640.
38. The Paulinus is perhaps 'Sextus Anicius Paulinus 15', *PLRE* I, pp. 679-80; and the Bassus, 'Iunius Bassus 14', *PLRE* I, pp. 154-5.
39. A Christian Gracchus was responsible for the destruction of a shrine of Mithras* while Prefect of the City of Rome in 376-7 ('Gracchus 1', *PLRE* I, p. 399).

eminent order of men create a country's character, these men do
so, when the will of the people is one with theirs and the common
people and the powerful are united. Look again at the illustrious
hall where sits the light of our state; only with difficulty will you
find a few minds still clouded with pagan frivolities, (575) tentatively
clinging to their worn-out rituals, choosing to keep to the darkness,
though it is banished, and shutting their eyes to the glorious noonday
sun.

## The piety of the Roman people (lines 578-86)

Now turn and look at the people. How few there are who do
not spurn Jupiter's* bloodstained altar. (580) All the crowd which
climbs to its tenement rooms or wears out the dark pavement with
its comings and goings or is fed by the bread dispensed at the high
steps — these people either throng to the tomb under the Vatican
hill where are buried the revered ashes of their father [Peter], given
in pledge and worthy of their love, (585) or in huge numbers
assemble at the Lateran palace where they receive the holy sign of
the Lord's anointing.[40]

## The pagan minority in the Senate (lines 587-642)

Do we still doubt that Rome is dedicated to you, Christ, that
she has passed under your laws and, with all her people and her
most eminent citizens, (590) wills to extend her earthly kingdom beyond the stars of the great and lofty heaven. I am not concerned
at the minute portion of mankind who keep their eyes closed to
daylight and stray from this course. Though outstanding for their services, noble in their blood, though they have earned high rewards
for their deserts in dignities and high office (595) and having reached
the top of the magisterial lists [i.e. as consul] have marked the record
of the annals with their names, though they are numbered among
the men of old in wax and bronze, yet the character of the country,
or the senate, does not depend on a small and contracting body
of men. (600) Whatever cause they cherish is held to by the private
will of a few scattered individuals, but the wishes of the people
oppose them and the resolution of the majority against them condemns their worried mutterings. If, in days of old, a senatorial resolution could stand (605) only if three hundred senators were on
record as having voted in agreement, let us keep to our ancestral
laws. Let the weak voice of the minority yield and fall silent in their
small part of the house.

See how, in a full senate, the men on our benches decree that
the city is to be purified (610) and the shameful couch of Jupiter*
and all idolatry exiled. A crowd crosses the house, as free in foot
as it is in heart, to the side to which the distinguished emperor's

---

40. For the Constantinian churches of the Lateran and the Vatican: D. Bowder,
    *The Age of Constantine and Julian*, London 1978, pp. 55-9.

decision calls them. There is no place for grudges, brute force intimidates no one. It is obvious that this is their will, a unanimous resolution of their judgement (615) not passed by order but following the convictions of reason alone.

Our good leader [Theodosius] gives a fair return for services in the earthly sphere to the worshippers of idols, grants them the highest honours and allows them to compete with the distinctions of their own families. (620) He does not forbid men entangled in the snares of paganism to rise to the highest worldly ranks where they are deserved, since divine affairs never stand in the way of earthly matters pursuing their accustomed course. He himself granted you [Symmachus] the consulship, the judgement-tribunal and endowed you with the gold-embroidered toga, he whose religion offends you (625) as the champion of doomed gods. You alone plead for the restoration of the deceits of Vulcan*, Mars* and Venus*, old Saturn's* stones, Phoebus'* ravings, the Ilian Mother's Megalensian festival*, the Bacchic orgies on Mount Nysa, the ridiculous rites of Isis* ever lamenting her lost Osiris*, which even her bald priests must laugh at, (630) and all the ghosts the Capitol, by tradition, shelters.

What a wonderful stream of eloquence flows from that tongue, O glory of Roman rhetoric, to whom Tully himself [Cicero] gives way! Yet these are the jewels which that rich store of eloquence pours out! (635) His mouth would deserve to be bathed in the radiance of gold eternal, had it but chosen to praise God! Yet [Symmachus] preferred his squalid monstrosities to Him, and polluted his clear voice with sin; (640) it was as if a man were to try to hoe muddy soil with an ivory rake, or dig in wet clay with a gold fork, when the black pitch dulls the brightness of the shining prongs and the keen, precious tool is caked over by filthy earth.

The Christian emperor survived his victory by only a few months. His death in Milan on 17 January 395 was followed by an outpouring of eulogies not only from Ambrose and Rufinus but also from Paulinus of Nola who praised Theodosius 'not so much as an emperor but as a servant of Christ, a man powerful not from the arrogance of rule but humility of service, a leader not through his kingly power but his faith'.[41] Paulinus also praised Theodosius' legislation.[42]

Ambrose's sermon on the death of Theodosius was preached in the cathedral at Milan, where the body of the emperor lay in state for forty days. The oration was delivered before an audience that included the new boy-emperor of the West, Honorius, his half-sister,

41.  Paulinus of Nola, *Epistula* (Letter) XXVIII.6.
42.  Jerome (to Paulinus), *Epistula* (Letter) LVIII.8.

Galla Placidia and the rising star of the Western court, Stilicho.

After this, the body was carried in slow procession eastward to Constantinople, escorted for the first stages of its journey by Honorius. On 8 November 395 Theodosius was finally laid to rest in the Church of the Holy Apostles beside Constantine and his other Christian predecessors.

---

Document 48: Ambrose, *De obitu Theodosii* (On the Death of Theodosius) 1, 2, 4, 6, 33, 39, 56

1.   Serious earthquakes and incessant rain threatened this calamity and a blackness deeper than the night gave us warning that the most merciful emperor Theodosius was about to depart from earth. Thus the very elements mourned his death, the sky was overcast with gloom, the atmosphere in a dreadful continual mist, the earth which was shaken by the earthquakes was deluged with floods. Was it not because the earth herself wept that she was suddenly deprived of her ruler, through whom the harshness of that world had been allayed, when pardon prevented the punishment for crime?

2.   So he has departed. Yet he has not resigned his kingdom but, by his being summoned by right of his holiness to the tabernacle of Christ, he has exchanged it for that heavenly Jerusalem, where he now dwells and tells us that 'I now see that of which I had formerly only heard in the city of the Lord of goodness, in the city of our God which "God founded to endure fovever".'

Still he has left very many behind him as if robbed of his fatherly protection, and chief among these are his own sons. Yet they are not truly deserted by him, for he has left them to be the heirs of his holiness . . .

4.   . . . We celebrate the *quadragesima* of Theodosius, who resembled the holy Jacob because he overthrew the treasonable attempt of the usurpers and concealed from sight the images of the pagans; for his faith had consigned to obscurity all the cults of the idols and abolished all their rites. He even grieved for those who had wronged him, sad that the pardon he had given was useless and the chance of showing mercy denied him . . .

[The inheritance of Theodosius' sons is intact and his will is honoured.]

6.   This great emperor, then, has left us, but he has not left us altogether. He leaves us his children in whom we should recognize himself and in whom we see him and hold him fast. Let not their youth influence you: for an emperor the trust of the soldiery is fullness of age. For fullness of age comes when virtue is mature. The two are linked together because the faith of the emperor is

also the courage of his soldiers.

7.   Think again, I ask, of the triumphs the faith of Theodosius won for you. When, because of the narrowness of the terrain and the servants' baggage, the army column came down to join battle a little late and it seemed the enemy would mount a successful cavalry charge because of the delay, the emperor jumped from his horse and advanced alone in front of the line saying, 'Where is the God of Theodosius?' He said this because of his closeness to Christ. Who could have said such a thing if he was not sure that he stood close to Christ? With these words he roused all his force, armed them with his example, advanced in age as he surely was but strong in his faith.

[Sections 8-12 concern the military exploits of Biblical heroes, 13-14 the mercy of Theodosius, 15-16 the fact that his sons are not too young to rule, 17-32 the virtues of Theodosius, stressing affection, kindness and humility, and the certainty of his salvation.]

33.   So, to conclude my address, I too loved the man who was merciful, humble in rule, gifted with a pure heart and a kindly spirit such as the Lord usually loves . . .

34.   I loved the man who showed himself more subject to reproof than to flattery. He laid down all the trappings of royal power he used and publicly in the church bewailed his sin, which he had incurred through the lies of others, and begged forgiveness with groans and tears. Private citizens are ashamed, but the emperor did not blush to do public penance and all the succeeding days brought him fresh remorse for his error. What of the occasion when he had won a glorious victory yet, because men had been slain in battle, he refrained from taking the sacraments until he had seen proof of God's favour to him in the arrival of his sons?

35.   I loved the man who asked for me in the last hours of his life with his last breath. I loved the man who, on the point of being released from the body, was more tormented by the state of his churches than his own perils . . .

[Sections 36-9 concern the certainty of the salvation of Theodosius.]

39.   Therefore Theodosius resides in the abode of light and glories among the bands of saints. There he embraces Gratian, no longer grieving over his wounds because he found his avenger: for though he was cut off by an unworthy death, he won rest for his soul. There both those good men, gifted with piety, generous with their compassion, enjoy the company of the other . . . On the opposite side, Maximus and Eugenius in Hell show 'as night unto night showeth knowledge'[43] by their tragic example how dire a thing

43.   Psalm 19.3.

it is to raise rebellion against their emperors. Of them it is well said,
'I have seen the wicked in great power and spreading himself on
high over the cedars of Lebanon. But I passed by, and, lo he was
not.'[44]

[Sections 40·9 describe Theodosius and his predecessors in
Heaven, including Constantine and his mother Helena, whose
discovery of the True Cross at Jerusalem is recounted. 50·2
describe the succession of pagan emperors by Christian ones
who find rest in heaven after their labours on earth. 54·5
describe the journey of the body to Constantinople.]

56. Do not fear that the relics of triumph will fail to receive
due honour wherever they arrive. Italy will not fail: she looked on
at his glorious triumphs and, liberated from usurpers a second time,
joins to praise the man who gave her freedom; nor will Constantinople, which for a second time sent an emperor to victory but could
not hold him back for herself, although she wished it. She looked
forward to triumphal festivities on his return, the sight of the inscriptions of his victories; she awaited an emperor of the whole world,
surrounded by the Gallic army, drawing on the strength of the whole
world. Yet it is a more powerful, a more glorious Theodosius who
returns to her now; a band of angels leads him home, an escort
of saints forms his guard of honour. Certainly blessed are you, Constantinople, who welcomes home a dweller in paradise and keeps
one who now lives in that city above as an honoured guest in his
body's burial place.

44.  Psalm 37.35·6.

# Chapter 4

# ANTI-PAGAN POLEMIC

To a Christian in the early years of Honorius' reign (395-423), the defeat of paganism seemed decisive. In this atmosphere of optimism it appeared an obvious truth that the Roman empire had been founded to further the empire of Christ, now triumphant, a theme found in Prudentius and echoed in the contemporary writings of Augustine and Jerome.[1]

Yet the political situation in the years following the death of Theodosius was not an easy one. Relations between the courts of Arcadius and Honorius were often strained, although open breaches between the brothers with their respective favourites were avoided. In Africa, Gildo, the Roman governor who was also a local prince, revolted in 397 and prevented the sailing of the vital corn ships to Rome and in Rome itself Symmachus, who had supported the Senate's declaration that Gildo was a public enemy, now found himself blamed for the resultant shortage.[2] The usurper was crushed, however, in 398. The Goths under Alaric advanced through Italy until in 402 they were defeated twice by Stilicho — at Pollentia, south of Turin, on 6 April, and at Verona in July or August of the same year.[3] The second book of Prudentius' *contra Symmachum* includes a long eulogy of the victory of Honorius and Stilicho at Pollentia, which may have been the poem's original inspiration.

These problems did not, however, impinge on the consciousness of Christian writers as a whole. The goddess of Victory still favoured the Christian cause. Prudentius could, with impunity, portray Arcadius and Honorius in their camp refuting the arguments of Symmachus. The issue of Victory was as crucial in 402 as it had been eighteen years before.

1.  For details: R. Markus, *Saeculum: History and Society in the Theology of St. Augustine*, Cambridge 1970.
2.  For the years 395-8: Alan Cameron, *Claudian. Poetry and Propaganda at the Court of Honorius*, Oxford 1970, pp. 63-155 and J. Matthews, *Western Aristocracies and Imperial Court*, Oxford 1975, pp. 253-83.
3.  Although our evidence for the battle of Verona (Claudian) is not easy to interpret, it points to the summer of 402 rather than 403 (Cameron, *Claudian. Poetry and Propaganda*, pp. 183-7).

Document 49: Prudentius, *Contra Symmachum* (Against Symmachus) II.17-38, 270-334, 640-772

## The Young Emperors' reply to Symmachus (lines 17-38)

At the end of the delegate's [Symmachus'] speech, the brother leaders [Arcadius and Honorius] calmly reply, 'We know how sweet victory is to the valiant, you most eloquent in the Ausonian tongue [Latin], (20) but we know, too, the methods and ways in which she is to be summoned. In our boyhood, our father gave us our first training in this skill, which he learned while a boy himself from the teaching of his own father. Victory does not come favourably when summoned by prayers or altars or pounded wheat; strenuous labour, rugged courage, (25) an outstanding force of mind, keenness, forcefulness and care; these, and brute strength in the handling of weapons, bring about victory. If warriors are without these, though a golden Victory spread her gleaming wings in a marble temple rising high, a figure costing many talents, yet she will not be at their side (30) and will appear to be offended at the withdrawal of their weapons. Why, soldier, distrust your own strength and equip yourself with useless assistance in the figure of a woman? No armoured legion ever saw a girl with wings come to direct the panting fighters' weapons. (35) Are you looking for the mistress of victory? It is a man's own right hand, and Almighty God, not a virago with combed hair, hovering bare-footed with a robe girded with a belt and flowing over swollen breasts.'

## The Christian theory of progress[4] (lines 270-334)

I want to know how you understand these teachings of the Father, most learned censor of the Italian race. Do you choose only old custom and abandon reason; does the keen intellect of a wise man allow of that statement that 'age-old custom has more weight with me (275) than the path of justice, the holiness revealed by heaven, faith in the truth, the rule of following correct belief?'

If we must piously reverence and preserve whatever custom was prevalent in the primitive years of the dawn of the world, (280) let us turn back the roll of the centuries to the beginning and resolve to condemn, step by step, all subsequent discoveries of successive experience. In the beginning, no ploughmen tilled the soil; what did they need ploughs for? or the wasteful labour of the harrow? It is better to fill one's belly with acorns from the oak trees. (285) Early men split their pliant timber with wedges, so let our axes be heated and melted down into a lump again and the distilled iron drip back

---

4.    For the ancient context of Prudentius' ideas on progress see E. R. Dodds, *The Ancient Concept of Progress and Other Essays in Greek Literature and Belief*, Oxford 1972, pp. 1-25.

into the ore from which it came. Slaughtered cows provided clothes, cold caves their mean homes; let us go back to our holes in the rock, (290) put on hairy garments of sewn hides. Let peoples who were once savage but had their ferocity subdued and became civilized now take to uttering their baleful howls again, go back to their wild ways and revert to their ancient habits. Let the young man with Scythian dutifulness (295) throw his father over the bridge in sacrifice (as was once the custom). Let Saturn's* altars steam with the sacrifice of murdered children, the cruel rites echoing with their tears and wailing. Let the people of Romulus weave houses of flimsy straw — such was the house Remus lived in, they say. (300) Let them spread hay on their royal beds and wear a cloak of Libyan bearskin on their hairy bodies. The Trinacrian general and the Tuscan had things like these.[5]

But Rome does not adhere to the way she was long ago but changes with time and alters her holy rites, ornaments, laws and weapons of war. (305) She observes many practices she did not observe in Quirinus' [Romulus'] reign: some of her enactments are better, some she has abandoned and she does not hesitate to change her custom and entirely reverses laws she formerly laid down. Why, senator of Rome, (310) do you bring up established usage against me, when often a resolution of senate and people has not stood but has been altered by a switch in sentiment. Even in our own day, whenever it is to our advantage to depart from habit and forfeit the usages of the past in favour of a fresh way of life, we rejoice at the new discovery of something at last revealed. (315) By constant slow changes does human life grow and increase, and profits from long experience.

Such are the changing stages of the age of man, the variations in his nature; in infancy he crawls; the child's step, like his mind, is weak and hesitant; (320) the hot blood of energetic youth burns. Soon comes the steady strength of the prime of life; and lastly old age, wiser in counsel but weaker in strength, declines physically although the mind is sound. By these same stages does mankind pass his changing life (325) through the contrasting generations. Dull in the first stages and sunk on the ground, he lived like a beast on all fours. Then, in childhood, his mind being teachable, he became refined by different new things. (330) Next he grew into passionate adolescence, swollen with vices, till he had burned out the excess of energy and matured in strength. Now the time has come to understand the divine and, with the greater activity of the unclouded spirit, to have the skill to search for the hidden mysteries and, at last, to take heed for eternal salvation.

## Speech of Rome to Arcadius and Honorius (lines 640-772)

For Rome does not grow old robbed of her former manly

---

5.   The 'Trinacrian general' was the Sicilian (Trinacria = Sicily) general, Acestes; the 'Tuscan' was Evander, the king of ancient Latium.

strength, nor does she feel the years. When wars summon her, it is not with shaking hands that she takes up her weapons, nor with such a feeble voice does she make her prayer to our honoured emperors as that most noble senator would have her do, (645) master of the art of words as he is, clever at inventing crafty arguments and putting on a false impression of a serious character, as an actor in a tragedy covers his face with a hollow wooden mask to breathe out some resounding profanity through its gaping mouth.

If one can invent a voice, certainly one more appropriate for Rome is the one I now put forward in her name. (650) She who thinks it shameful to weep for the rejection of the temples or assert that an aegis fought for her in times of crisis, or admit that she is bowed by the weight of years, joyfully honours and addresses her leaders (655) as follows:

'I greet you, famous leaders, noble offspring of an unconquered emperor under whose rule I was reborn and completely cast off old age and saw my grey hairs turn to gold again: for though age reduces all mortal things, my length of days has brought me to new life and, (660) by my long survival, I have learned to despise death. Now, now at last I have proper respect paid to my years and I now deserve to be called "venerable" and capital of the world when I shake my helmet with its scarlet crest under its olive leaves, my stern sword-belt wreathed with a green garland, (665) though in full armour, I worship God without the taint of blood. Alas, to my sorrow, cruel Jupiter* urged me on to bloodshed, so that I was stained by the sacred blood of the virtuous and desecrated by murder, a weapon accustomed to war. At his prompting Nero was the first, after slaying his mother, (670) to drink the blood of the apostles, polluting me with the murder of holy men, and in his cruelty to brand the shame of his own wickedness on me.[6] After him, Decius,[7] too, frenzied with slaughter, fed his mad rage. Soon a similar thirst burned fiercely in many others avid (675) to draw out noble souls through severe wounds and toy with punishments. It poured a flood of corpses into my lap and cut off the heads of the guiltless by sentence of the courts. Now your times have purified me of this sin. (680-3) . . .

'There are some, too, who do not hesitate to reproach us for reverses in war, since we rejected the temples' altars and claim that African Hannibal was repulsed from the juncture of the Colline Gate by the power of Jupiter* and Mars*, and the conquering Senones routed from the Capitol, because divine powers fought from the rock high above! (690) Let those who shout at me about a past disaster

---

6.   The emperor Nero (54-68) was responsible not only for murdering his mother Agrippina in 59 but for executing Christians as scapegoats for the great fire at Rome in 64.
7.   The emperor Decius (249-51) launched a systematic persecution of Christians in 250.

and old griefs yet again see that in your time I suffer none of these: no barbarian enemy shakes my barricades with his spear or wanders, with his outlandish weapons, clothes and hair, at will all over the city he has captured, (695) carrying off my youth to captivity across the Alps.

'Recently a Gothic usurper [Alaric] tried to destroy Italy: he came from his native Danube under oath to raze these strongholds to the ground, give these golden roofs over to the flames and dress our toga-clad leaders in animal skins. (700) Already in his assault he had trampled down the fields of Venetia with his squadrons and laid waste rich Liguria and the delightful countryside by the deep waters of the Po; crossing the river he descended on the lands of Tuscany. It was no watchful goose that drove away that cavalry storm revealing a danger concealed in the shadows of night, (705) but the physical force of warriors, the crash of breast on breast in battle, a spirit that did not fear to die for its country and seek glorious acclaim through its wounds. Did that day, too, grant its high reward for bravery through Jupiter's* favour? The leader of our army, as of our empire, was a young man [Honorius] (710) powerful in Christ and his companion and father, Stilicho, with Christ the one God for both. After they had worshipped at his altars and had the cross imprinted on their foreheads, the trumpets sounded. First, ahead of the dragon standards, a spear advanced to carry the crest of Christ high above them. (715) There a race that for thirty years had been the ruin of Pannonia finally paid the price with its destruction.

'The bodies of men once enriched by notorious plundering lie gathered into heaps. In later ages, posterity, you will marvel at the corpses lying unburied far and wide (720) which cover with their bones the plains of Pollentia. If, after being sacked at the hands of the Gauls, I could raise my head from the filthy ashes, if, on Camillus' return, I could welcome my standards with a smiling face, although the smoke still hung, if I could wreathe my sad ruins with garlands (725) and place necklaces of bay leaves around my tottering towers, how shall I feel as I welcome you, most valiant emperor? What flowers shall I scatter? What garlands shall I use to drape my halls? What hanging shall I place over my doors to celebrate, seeing that I am untouched by this great war, (730) free while you are under arms, the rumour of the Goths' onset barely reaching my ears? Enter your triumphal chariot, gather up your spoils and, with Christ at your side, come home to me. Let me remove the chains from the crowds of prisoners, lay aside the fetters worn smooth during your long servitude, you bands of mothers and men. (735) Let the exile from his family home forget slavery in his old age, and the child learn to know he is free-born as his mother returns to her father's house. Let all fear depart. We have won: it is time to celebrate. What success like this did we gain from the defeat of the Punic general long ago? (740) After he had broken with his blows the shaken bolts of a gate he attacked, he relaxed in the waters of Baiae and his toughness and strength were lost through self-indulgence, his sword broken by lust. But our Stilicho fought the enemy hand to hand and forced him to flee from the very heat of battle. (745) This time Christ our God and plain courage were on our side; formerly it was your delights, luxuriant Campania, that conquered a licentious enemy — Jupiter* did not shield the bold Fabius but lovely Tarentum aided him by allowing him to trample underfoot a despot already conquered by her allurements.[8] (750) I [Rome] do not have the means to give you a reward great enough for this deliverance ... (756) To you, our emperor, a living glory is due, a living reward for your bravery, since you sought deathless honour. You will be the partner of Christ in the rule of the world forever, for under his leadership you raise my empire to the stars (760).

'Do not, I beg, be swayed by the voice of the great orator [Symmachus], who, in the role of ambassador, bemoans the death of his rites and with the weapons of his intellect and the powers of his eloquence dares, alas, to attack our faith, not realizing that you, Augustus, and I have devoted ourselves to that God in whose name (765) we have closed their foul temples and overturned their blood-soaked altars. Let Christ alone be king and keep our palaces safe, let all demons be strangers to the towers of Romulus and my court serve the Prince of Peace and no other.'

With these words Rome convinced her devout sons (770) to reject the ambassador's unacceptable request, for he came as ambassador from a seer in Jupiter's* sanctuary, not from his country: his country's true glory is Christ.

Many instances of anti-pagan polemic cannot be dated with any certainty to the period 395-410 because the themes of the debate remained to a large extent constant. In the anti-pagan literature of the time the contemporary sources of conflict appear submerged under a cloud of archaism and antiquarianism. The defenders of paganism resurrected old arguments from the second and third centuries while the Christians often turned their attacks on pagan works of an even earlier date: thus Augustine for example devotes a large part of the earlier chapters of the *City of God* to attacking the Roman republican writer, Varro.[9]

Yet the tracing of echoes of Tertullian and other past masters of anti-pagan polemic gives only part of the picture. The conflict was not only literary but political and social. On the literary level, the battle was fought in terms of past precedents because the past, both culturally and historically, was itself an issue. Many Christians

---

8.   The Roman general Fabius Cunctator ('The Delayer') was responsible for blunting the successes of Hannibal in Italy. Tarentum had been recaptured by 209 BC.

9.   R. Markus, 'Paganism, Christianity and the Latin Classics' in J. Binns (ed.), *Latin Literature of the Fourth Century*, London 1974, pp. 1-21.

felt that Christian culture was incompatible with continued interest in the pagan classics: hence Jerome reproached himself for being a follower of Cicero rather than of Christ[10] and Paulinus of Nola, in renouncing the use of pagan themes in his poetry, declared that 'hearts dedicated to Christ deny the pagan muses and are closed to Apollo'.[11]

Such writers as these attempted to resolve the cultural tension between Christian themes and the continued use of pagan language, and were often more bitter against lukewarm Christians than their pagan opponents. Meanwhile others took issue over the role of God or the gods in history, particularly in the history of Rome, as has been seen, a debate in which *exempla* from the past were crucial to both sides. The use of examples to illustrate or prove a point was a basic part of the rhetorical training that formed the educational background of the Christian apologists as well as of their pagan opponents. A large element of the conventional would not only be expected from a man educated in this fashion but would be essential if he was to make himself understood.

All the examples of anti-pagan polemic that follow are believed to derive from the period prior to the sack of Rome in 410. This event was a symbolic catastrophe and radically changed the lines on which the Christian-pagan debate was to be conducted. No more is heard after 410 of the historical optimism inherent in Christian theories of progress towards a Christian empire. In Augustine's *City of God*, the Christian was invited to turn his eyes from the secular Rome, which could fall in time, to the Eternal Rome in heaven, while Orosius' *History against the Pagans* argued that Rome had been even more subject to disasters when guided by her pagan gods.

One of the most curious specimens of anti-pagan polemic is the anonymous *Carmen contra paganos*, which survives only in a single manuscript, attached to a Paris manuscript of Prudentius (Cod. Par.Lat.8084), dated to the year 527. This very difficult poem, the text of which is exceptionally corrupt, is an invective directed against an unnamed prefect and consul for his public participation in pagan ceremonies. He has been variously identified as Vettius Agorius Praetextatus (d.384) and Gabinius Barbarus Pompeianus (d.408). However, it seems most likely that the poem is addressed to Nicomachus Flavianus (d.394), hence it is sometimes entitled 'A Poem against Flavianus'.[12]

---

10. Jerome, *Epistula* (Letter) XXII.30.
11. Paulinus of Nola, *Carmen* (Poem) X.21-2.
12. The original identification of Flavianus was established by T. Mommsen, 'Car-

## Document 50: Anonymous, *Carmen contra paganos* (Poem against the Pagans)

Tell me, you people who worship the sacred groves and cave of the Sibyl* and the thicket of Ida*; the lofty Capitol of thundering Jupiter*, the Palladium and the household gods [Lares*] of Priam, the chapel of Vesta*,[13] and the incestuous gods, the sister married to her brother,[14] the cruel boy [Cupid*], the statues of unspeakable Venus*, (5) you whom only the purple toga consecrates, you to whom the oracle of Phoebus* has never spoken true, you whom the delusive Etruscan diviner forever mocks; this Jupiter* of yours, overwhelmed with love for Leda, did he mean to cover himself with white feathers so as to change into a swan, when desperately in love to flow all at once to Danae as a golden shower, (10) to bellow through the straits of Parthenope [Naples] as an adulterous bull? If these monstrous rites find favour are no hallowed things modest? Is the ruler of Olympus [Saturn*] forced to retreat, in flight from the arms of Jupiter? (15) And does any suppliant venerate the temples of the tyrant, when he sees the father compelled to fight by his own son? Finally, if Jupiter* himself is ruled by Fate what advantage is it to wretched men to pour forth prayers already foredoomed? The handsome young man, Adonis*, is mourned in the temples, (20) naked Venus* weeps, Mars* the hero rejoices, Jupiter* in the middle does not know how to bring about reconciliation and Bellona* urges on the quarrelling gods with her whip.

Is it fitting for senators to hope for safety from sacred leaders such as these? Should they be allowed to settle your quarrels? Tell me, what benefit to the City was your prefect, when, a plunderer in ceremonial attire, he had reached the throne of Jupiter*[15], whereas [in fact] he scarcely atones for his crimes by a protracted death? This man who feverishly purified the whole city for three months finally came to the limits of his life. (30) What madness of spirit was this, what insanity of mind? He was certainly able to disturb your

---

*Footnote 12 continued*

    men Codicis Parisini 8084', *Hermes*, 4, 1870, pp. 350-63 (= *Gesammelte Schriften*, VII, pp. 485-98). However, in recent times the poem has been associated with the Prefect of the City of Rome in 408-9, Pompeianus, by G. Manganaro, 'La reazione pagana a Roma nel 408-9 d. C. e il poemetto anonimo *contra paganos*', *Giornale Italiano di Filologia*, 13, 1960, pp. 210-24. The case for Flavianus has been restated, with more detailed argumentation, by J. Matthews, 'The Historical Setting of the *carmen contra paganos* (Cod. Par. Lat. 8084)', *Historia*, 20, 1970, pp. 464-79. The poem still deserves closer analysis in the general context of the anti-pagan polemic at the time.

13.   The Palladium, Lares* and Vesta* were normally preserved together in the one temple.

14.   A reference to Juno's* marriage to Jupiter*, a common butt of Christian jibes.

15.   Compare Document 67, p. 107 for the boast of the wife of Praetextatus.

Jupiter's* peace! Who, most beautiful Rome, provoked your suspension of public business?[16] Was the populace, long since a stranger to them, to resort to arms?

But there was no one on earth more hallowed than he (35) whom Numa Pompilius*, the chief diviner among many, taught by an empty rite outrageously to pollute the altars in the blood of cattle with putrefying carcasses.[17] Is this not the very same man who once betrayed the wine of his country[18] and ancient households, overturning the towers and residences of the nobility (40), since he wished to bring destruction on his city, adorned his doorposts with laurel, gave banquets, offered unclean bread tainted with the smoke of incense, asking in jest whom he would give over to death, who was ever accustomed to put on the sacred garments (45), forever ready to corrupt the unfortunate with some new deceit?

How, I ask you, did your priest help the city? He taught the [Greek] priest to seek the Sun beneath the earth,[19] and when a grave-digger from the countryside happened to cut down a pear tree for himself, would say that he was a companion of the gods and mentor of Bacchus*, (50) he, a worshipper of Serapis*, always a friend to the Etruscan diviners, the one who sought eagerly to pour for the unwary his draughts of poison, who sought a thousand ways of harming and as many contrivances. Those whom he wished to ruin he struck down — the ghastly snake! — ready as he was to fight the true God, in vain (55), he who always mourned in silence the times of peace, unable to proclaim his own deep grief.

Which initiate of the *taurobolium** persuaded you to change your clothes so that you, a puffed-up rich man, should suddenly become a beggar covered in rags and having been made a pauper[20] by your small contribution (60) sent underground, stained with bull's blood, dirty, corrupted, to preserve your bloodied garments and hope to live pure for twenty years?[21] You set yourself up as a censor to cut down the life of your betters, henceforth trusting that your own actions would lie hidden, although you had always been surrounded with the dogs of the Great Mother*,[22] (65) you whom the

16. The term *iustitium* is a technical one, normally taken to mean the proclamation of a state of emergency to cope with internal turmoil.
17. This refers to the augural ritual and the feast of the Parentalia (Prudentius, *Contra Symmachum* [Against Symmachus] II.1107-8).
18. This is apparently an allusion to some tampering with the wine supply during the City prefecture of Flavianus in 383 (Mommsen, 'Carmen Codicis Parisini 8084', p. 363).
19. A reference to the rite of Mithras* whereby Attis* becomes the Sun-god.
20. The word translated is *epaeta* which occurs nowhere else in Latin literature and is probably an adoption of the Greek *epaites* (beggar). It may refer, as a technical term, to a grade of initiate of the cult of Mithras*.
21. The initiation of the *taurobolium** was normally meant to last for twenty years according to contemporary inscriptions from Rome (e.g. *CIL* VI. 502, 504, 512).
22. A reference to the dog masks worn at the festival of the Great Mother*, the

licentious band (O horror!) accompanied in your triumph. The old man of sixty remained a boy,[23] a worshipper of Saturn*, constant friend of Bellona*, who persuaded everyone that the Fauns*, (70) companions of the nymph Egeria,[24] and the Satyrs* and Pans* are gods. He is a companion of nymphs and Bacchus* and priest of Trivia,[25] whom the Berecynthian Mother* inspired to lead the choral dances, take up the staffs of effeminacy[26] and clash the cymbals; whom powerful Galatea [Venus*], born of lofty Jove and endowed with (75) the prize of beauty through the judgement of Paris,[27] commanded. Let no priest be allowed to keep his shame when they are in the habit of chanting in falsetto in the Megalensian celebrations. Thus in his madness he wanted to damn many worshippers of Christ were they willing to die outside the Law, and would give honours to those he would ensnare, through demonic artifice, (80) forgetful of their true selves, seeking to influence the minds of certain people by gifts and to make others profane with a small bribe and send the wretched people below with him to Hell. He who wanted pious agreements to replace the laws had (85) Leucadius[28] put in charge of the African farms, to corrupt Marcianus[29] so that he might be his proconsul.

What was the divine custodian of Paphos [Venus*], the matron Juno* and elderly Saturn* able to provide for you, their priest? What did the trident of Neptune* promise you, O madman? (90) What responses could the Tritonian maiden [Minerva*] give? Tell me, why did you seek the temple of Serapis* by night? What did deceitful Mercury* promise you as you went? What do you gain from having worshipped the Lares* and two-faced Janus*? What pleasure to you as priest did our parent Earth give, or the beautiful mother of the gods? (95) What barking Anubis*; what the pitiable mother Ceres*,

---

*Footnote 22 continued*

Megalensia*. For similar instances: Carmen ad senatorem (Poem to a senator) line 31 (= Document 51, p. 84) and Carmen ad Antonium (Poem to Antonius) lines 117–18 (= Document 52, p. 89).

23.  The word efebus here may refer to a grade of worship of the cult of Hercules.

24.  Egeria is said to have suggested to Numa* all his wise laws.

25.  Bacchus* = Liber*, Trivia = Hecate*. Such dedications are common in fourth-century inscriptions.

26.  Staffs wound around with vines and topped with a pine cone were used in the ceremony of Bacchus*.

27.  Paris was asked which of the three goddesses should receive the golden apple dedicated 'to the most beautiful'. Hera offered him fame, Athena offered him military glory, but he chose Aphrodite (Venus*), who offered him the world's loveliest woman.

28.  Leucadius was an imperial financial official in Africa at the time. See 'Leucadius 2', PLRE I, p. 505.

29.  Marcianus became Prefect of the City of Rome in 409. After the defeat of Eugenius and Arbogast in September 394 Marcianus was compelled to pay back the salary he had acquired as Flavianus' pronconsul in Africa ('Marcianus 14', PLRE I, pp. 555–6 and Document 90, p. 119).

and Proserpine* below; what lame Vulcan*, weak in one foot? Who did not laugh at your grieving, whenever you came bald to the altars as a suppliant to beseech rattle-bearing Faria [Isis*] and when, after lamentation, you carried the broken olive branch (100) when mourning wretched Osiris*, [as Isis] sought the one she would lose again when found? We have seen lions bearing yokes wrought in silver,[30] when joined together they pulled creaking wooden wagons, and we have seen (105) that man holding silver reins in both his hands. We have seen eminent senators following the chariot of Cybele* which the hired band dragged at the Megalensian festival, carrying through the city a lopped-off tree trunk,[31] and suddenly proclaiming that castrated Attis* is the Sun.[32] (110) While through your magic arts, alas, you seek the honours of princes, pitiable man, you are thereby brought low with the gift of a small tomb. Yet only the promiscuous Flora* rejoices in your consulship, the shameful mother of games and mistress of Venus*, to whom but recently your heir Symmachus[33] constructed a temple. (115) You, stationed in the temple, continually worshipped all those monstrous things while your suppliant wife with her hands heaps up the altars with grain and gifts and prepares to fulfil her vows to the gods and goddesses on the threshold of the temple, and threatens the divine powers, desiring to sway Acheron* with magic verses, (120) yet sent him wretched headlong down to Tartarus. Leave off weeping after such a spouse, a sufferer from dropsy, he whose wish was to hope for salvation from Latian Jupiter*.

A similar poem is included in the works of the third-century African bishop, Cyprian, though it is clearly not by him. It has been dated to the late fourth century on account of its close resemblances in style and content to the *Poem against the Pagans* (Document 50) and the poem to Antonius (Document 52) and is addressed to an unidentified apostate consul, whose relapse is discussed in the context of both polemic against pagan ritual and contemporary Christian doctrines of repentance and redemption.

30. Representations of the lions of Cybele* can be found on contemporary tokens (*contorniates*) and tapestries. For details see M. Vermaseren, *Cybele and Attis*, London 1977, pp. 96ff.
31. The pine trunk was carried in procession through the city on 22-23 March each year (ibid., p. 115).
32. Attis* was declared the Sun at the annual feast of the Hilaria, held on 25 March.
33. This refers to the younger Flavianus who had married the daughter of Symmachus (Matthews, 'Historical Setting', p. 477), rather than Symmachus' son ('Q. Fabius Memmius Symmachus 10', *PLRE* II, p. 1047).

Document 51: Pseudo-Cyprian, *Carmen ad senatorem ex Christiana religione ad idolorum servitutem conversum* (Poem to a Senator converted from Christianity to the service of idols)

When I saw you paying homage once again to a variety of empty sacred objects and clinging to your former error, I was dumbfounded. Because you always enjoyed poetry, I have hastened to write verses so that by replying in a poem (5) I shall reproach you. For who may allow darkness to be preferred to light or that you should believe that the Great Mother* could be said to be a goddess and think that she whose devotees are branded by scandalous infamy may be worshipped again? For indeed the priests in effeminate garb (10) confess to their same private vice in public ritual, and think admissible that which is not. Whereupon they mince lightly through the city speaking in feminine voices and carry themselves with languishing hips and finger extended, and change their sex through a well publicized crime. (15) And when they celebrate their rites they proclaim that on these days they are chaste. Yet if only then are they, as they say, chaste, then what are they for the rest of the time? But because they are compelled to be pure at least once, they groan in spirit, disfigure their body and shed their blood. (20) What holy rite indeed is it which goes by the name of blood? For I have now learnt that not age but your religion has made you bald, that your [Roman] boots are removed and your feet swathed in the soft papyrus of the Galli — an object quite astonishing and this could be thrown down from a great height. (25) If any consul proceeds into the city from the rite of Isis* he will be the laughing-stock of the world:[34] who, however, will not mock that you who were consul are now a minister of Isis*? What is shameful in the first instance you are not ashamed to be in the second: to abuse your mind through vile hymns (30) with the rabble responding to you and the senate censuring you; and, once depicted in your home with the *fasces*, now to bear a dog-like countenance with your rattle.[35] Is this humility? It is but a semblance of humility. Those monuments will always remain part of your house. (35) And the general rumour abroad had reached our ears that you have said: 'Goddess, I was mistaken, forgive me, I have returned'. Tell me, if you please, since you often made these requests and sought forgiveness, what words does she say to you? You, who follow those who are mindless, are truly deprived of your wits. (40) Once again you seek out these things and do not realize that you are doing wrong. See what you deserve. Perhaps you would have been less notorious if you had known only this and persisted in this error. Yet, since you

34.   Although the text reads *oris*, we think *orbis* makes better sense.
35.   The ritual masks of the rites of the Great Mother*.

have crossed the threshold of the true Law and come to know God for a few years, (45) why do you cling to what should be abandoned or why do you give up what should be retained? When you worship everything, you worship nothing. Nor do you reconsider in your heart how different is truth from falsehood, light from darkness. You only pretend to be a philosopher since opinion changes your mind. For if popular anger prompted your displeasure (50) you would be both a Jew and be held to be uncertain of everything. Indulge yourself with words, lofty wisdom does not satisfy. All that is carried to excess, fails: heat and cold have the same effect, the former burns and so does the latter. So darkness brings light and the sun the opposite; (55) the icy cold and the boiling hot bath are equally harmful. Food sustains the body, the body is corrupted by food and decreases its own strength, if too much is consumed. Lastly, if you sit it is a great rest from work: but if you sit for long it becomes a strain. For the poet Virgil (60) described as a punishment: 'Unfortunate Theseus sits and will sit forever'.[36] Length always harms something useful: lengthy banquets are harmful, long fasts are trying. Likewise, knowing too much makes you stupid.

'The wicked sect, so the goddess taught me, said moderation was good.' (65)

But you care for neither principle nor the guidance of the mean. However, a stable mind is not thrown off course by any turmoil and simplicity itself never contemplates any evil. Wherefore, sincere faith shall enjoy an eternal abode and wrongdoing on the other hand will be tortured in lasting fire. (70) Choose what you wish in order to avoid deserved punishments. I say nevertheless that the creditor deserves this concession. If you do not wish to know the truth, the offence will be light. It will not be light if you abandon the truth already known. But perhaps mature old age will recall you (75), when you are sated with these errors, to correction and the better path. For time changes evil, time sets everything in order. Therefore, then, when age and experience have restored you, learn to keep faith with God, lest you happen to lapse the same way a second time, because it is truly said (80) that he who has once tripped over a stone and is not aware of how to avoid it and carelessly hurts himself a second time must ascribe blame to himself, and not to other causes. Correct your sin with faith, straighten out your mind. It was sufficient to sin once. Leave off fearing. He who repents of what he previously was will not be held to account.

A third anti-pagan invective is the 'Poem to Antonius', which has been preserved by chance in two manuscripts of Paulinus of Nola and is accepted by some as his. Others maintain that investigation

36.  *Aeneid* VI.617.

of other religions is inconsistent with Paulinus' commitment to Christianity from birth and that the authorship is unknown.[37]

---

### Document 52: Pseudo-Paulinus, *Carmen* XXXII: *Carmen ad Antonium* (Poem to Antonius) 1-164

I admit to having examined all ways of belief, Antonius; I have enquired into much, run through questions in every detail, yet I have found nothing superior to belief in Christ. Now I have arranged to set this out in flowing verse and, to avoid offence in my choice of poetic subject, I cite David himself who prayed to God through the poetry he sang, as my precedent for treating great matters with humble words. I shall speak of what should be shunned, followed, or worshipped, although both practice and its principles must be established in all things.

(10) In the first place, even the marvellous favour of God did not influence the Jewish race; for, when they were rescued from the wicked Pharaoh and crossed the sea on foot with their leader, the pillar of light shining before them, they saw the enemy cavalry overwhelmed by the waters. Although they had left cultivated fields behind them, they never lacked anything, as manna fell from the sky and springs gushed from the rock, yet, after all these great things, they denied the present help of God and, while seeking another divinity in the madness of their hearts, lit fires and lost the gold that he had sent.

The pagan, too, is the same. He worships stones he has carved himself (20) and creates by his own hand the object to which he owes fear. Then he adores images which he has so moulded from bronze that he can melt them down for coin whenever he wants to, or change them, as he often does, into shapes he should be ashamed of. Hence he sacrifices unfortunate cattle and looks in their warm lungs for the intentions of the gods (25) whom he believes angry, and prays for the life of a man through the death of a beast. What kind of forgiveness can a man ask who asks it with blood? What a strange, stupid damnable practice it is! After the omnipotent God once formed man (30) man dares to fashion God; to complete the tally of sin, he also sells the image and the buyer purchases himself a master.

Could I accept that philosophers' beliefs are reasonable when they are unreasonable themselves, they whose wisdom is but vain? There are the dog-like Cynics — their name betrays them. (35) Some follow the dogma of Plato, who doubted it himself, and worry themselves over the composition of the soul, a matter discussed now

---

37.   For this poem, and its relationship to the other two: C. Morelli, 'L'Autore del cosidetto *Poema ultimum* attribuito a Paolino di Nola', *Didaskaleion*, I, 1912, pp. 481-98.

for a long time past. They investigate it constantly yet are never able to reach a conclusion, which is why they like copying Plato's book on the soul, a book containing nothing susceptible of proof apart from the title.[38] (40) There are also the Physici, so called from the word for nature, who enjoy living in an old-fashioned, uncultivated and uncouth fashion. For there was once a man[39] who carried only a staff and a pottery dish, because they were, he thought, the only indispensably useful things, hence the only possessions one should have, the one to support him, the other to drink out of. (45) But when he saw a farmer standing and drinking water out of his cupped hands, he smashed his dish and threw it away from him saying that one should reject all superfluous things. A country man had taught him that one could reject that small dish too. These men neither drink wine, nor do they eat bread, (40) nor lie on a bed nor wear clothes to keep out the cold and, in their ingratitude to God, refuse what he has offered them.

What can I say of the various religious rites and temples set up to gods and goddesses? Let me first talk of the character of the Capitol; they have a god and a god's wife and (55) will have it that she is his sister, as Virgil, their creator, denoted by his phrase 'both sister and wife'. It is also said of Jupiter* that he violated his daughter and gave her to his brother and, to get other women, changed his shape; now he was a snake, now a bull, now a swan and a tree (60) and by all these changes provided his own evidence as to his real nature, preferring the shapes of others to his own. Even more disgraceful than this, he pretended to be an eagle and accepted the unnatural embraces of a boy.[40] What do his crowd of worshippers say? Let them either deny this is Jupiter* or admit his unseemly conduct. (65) He certainly has a prestige not confirmed by reasoned thought. They make sacrifices to Jupiter* and call him 'Jupiter the Best' and make requests to him and also place 'Father Janus' in the first rank of gods. This Janus* was a king long ago[41] who named the Janiculan hill after himself, a wise man who (foresaw) as many things in the future (70) as he could look back (on in the past) and so the ancient Latins pictured him with two faces and called him the two-headed Janus*. Because he had arrived in Italy in a boat, the first coin was struck in honour of him with the following devices: (75) on one side was carved a head, on the other, a ship. It is in

---

38. This was Plato's *Phaedo* in which Socrates, about to die, discusses the nature of the soul and the after-life.
39. Diogenes the Cynic (died about 324 BC). He called himself the 'Dog' (Cynic), thinking that animals lived a model life, and advocated this extreme indifference to material goods.
40. Ganymede, the son of a king of Troy, was kidnapped by Jupiter* and taken to be his cup-bearer on Olympus.
41. The argument that the gods were originally men goes back to the Greek philosopher, Euhemerus, in the third century BC. It is given lengthy treatment by Prudentius, *Contra Symmachum* (Against Symmachus) I.42-277.

memory of this that men distinguish the sides of some of their coins, calling one side 'heads' and the other 'ships' after that event long ago. Why do they hope for anything from Jupiter* who came second after this king yet who is served with offerings through the lips of suppliants? (80) This god has a mother, too, who was overtaken by love for a shepherd, so the shepherd himself came before Jupiter* or Jove; but the shepherd was his superior for, wishing to preserve his chastity, he rejected the goddess who in her rage castrated him so that he (85) who had refused to come to her bed should never be the husband of another.[42] Was this the just ordinance of the gods however, that a man who had not been made a fornicator should never be a husband? Now, too, eunuchs chant shameful mysteries nor are there lacking men to be corrupted by this infection. (90) They worship some secret the more profound for being behind closed doors and call holy something which would render a modest man unholy should he approach it. Thus the priest himself, more restricted, avoids sleeping with women and accepts the embrace of men.

O blinded intellect of man! Plays about their holy things (95) always arouse laughter, yet they do not abandon the error of their ways. They maintain Saturn* was Jupiter's* father and that first he devoured his children and then vomited up his unspeakable meal, yet later, by a trick of his wife's, he swallowed a stone, believing it to be Jupiter* and that (100) if he had not done that, Jupiter* would have been consumed. They call Saturn* Chronus and give him this name, meaning Time, because he swallows the time he creates and then brings up again what he has swallowed. But why be so devious in inventing a name for Time? Moreover, this god, who always so feared his children's designs for himself, (105) when hurled out of heaven by Jupiter*, lay latent in the fields of Italy, called Latium for that reason. What great gods they both were! One hid under the earth, the other could not know the earth's hiding places. Therefore the Quirites [Romans] established the evil rite of Latiaris, (110) using human sacrifice to glut an empty name. How deep is the night of the mind, how unthinking the human heart! The object of their worship is nothing, yet the rites cause the shedding of blood.

What of the fact that they hide the Unconquered One in a rocky cave and dare to call the one they keep in darkness the Sun?[43] (115) Who adores light in secret or hides the star of the sky in the shadows beneath the earth except for some evil purpose? Why do they not hide the rites of Isis* with her symbols and the dog-headed Anubis* even deeper, instead of showing them throughout the public places as they do? Yes, they look for something and rejoice when they have found it (120) and lose it again so that they can hunt for it again. What sensible man could put up with the sight of one sect hiding the sun, as it were, while the others openly display their mon-

42. A version of the story of Cybele* and Attis*.
43. Mithras* is often entitled 'Unconquered' on inscriptions.

strous gods? What had Serapis* done to deserve to be so dragged
and torn by his own people through such varied and degrading
places? Always at last he (125) becomes a wild beast, a dog, a
decomposing ass's corpse, he becomes now a man, now bread, now
heavy with disease. While acting in this way, they admit he feels
nothing.

What should I say too of Vesta*, when her own priest says he
does not know what she is? Yet deep in the heart of her sanctuary
(130) they claim there is preserved the undying fire. Why is she a
goddess, not a god? Why is fire [masculine in Latin] called a woman?
Yet Vesta* was a woman, so Hyginus[44] implies, who was the first
to weave a garment from new thread, called a 'vestment' from her
name, which she gave (135) to Vulcan* who, in return, showed her
how to watch over her hidden hearths; Vulcan*, in his turn, was
pleased with the gift and offered it to the Sun, by whose help he
had previously discovered the adultery of Mars*;[45] nowadays all the
credulous mob at the Vulcanalia hang up garments for the Sun. (140)
To show the character of Venus*, Adonis*[46] is carried out; then they
send for manure and throw it about him. If you look into everything,
it becomes more and more laughable. There is this additional detail:
I gather that every five years the so-called Vestal Virgins* take a
feast to a serpent who either does not exist at all, or else is the
Devil himself, (145) who formerly persuaded the human race to its
ruin. But they venerate him, even though now he trembles and hangs
imprisoned by the name of Christ and confesses to his evil deeds.
How strange is the mind of man that he tells lies instead of the
truth, (150) worships what he should renounce and turns his back
on what he should adore.

Now I shall have said enough about useless fears. Before I saw
the clear light, I too was uncertain on all these things for a long
time, tossed by many a storm, but the holy church received me into
a harbour of safety (155) and set me in a peaceful anchorage after
my wanderings over the waves, so that the dark clouds of evil might
be dispersed and, at the promised time, I might hope for the calm
light of heaven. For that former salvation, which the forgetful Adam
lost when urged off course by an adverse wind, now, with Christ
at the oar, (160) is pushed off the rocks and arises once more to
remain with us forever. For he, our helmsman, so guides all things
everywhere that he who but recently removed our mistaken thinking
now sets us on a better road and opens the gates of Paradise. Fortunate is our faith in its dedication to a sure and single God.

---

44. Hyginus was a second-century author who compiled, mainly from Greek
    sources, a handbook of mythology (Genealogiae).
45. Mars* committed adultery with Venus*, the wife of Vulcan*, who caught them
    in the act by dropping a net over the bed.
46. Venus* was in love with Adonis*, who rejected her advances and was later
    killed by a boar while hunting.

Like Prudentius (see Documents 5 and 54), Paulinus of Nola believed in the power of martyrs to help in the fight against paganism. The following extract is taken from his poem to St Felix of 405.

## Document 53: Paulinus of Nola, *Carmen* (Poem) XIX.84-158

Mark [the apostle] was given to you, Alexandria[47], in order to (85) rout the bull, along with Jupiter*, so that Egypt should no longer worship cattle in the shape of Apis[48] nor the Cretans offer false honours to an entombed man, believing him to be Jupiter.[49] No more will the Phrygians celebrate the rites of Cybele* with the eunuch Galli, her priests, propitiating the corrupt mother-goddess with shameful self-mutilation, so that at last the trees produce pure foliage on Ida's peaks (90) and the pines are not touched by guilt on heights now free of fear. Nor any longer shall Greece consult in vain the silent oracle of Delphi but despise and trample down their own Olympus as they mount up to Sion, where on the high summit Christ shall press his easy yoke upon his child's neck. (95) From Ephesus too is Diana put to flight by the onset of the apostle John, in company with her brother Apollo* whom Paul, the conqueror of Pytho, has routed by orders issued in the name of Christ.[50] Satan flees from Egypt too, where he had taken a thousand shapes (100) and a thousand names, disguising himself as a variety of monsters ... With the aim of abolishing these profane honours, the hidden purpose of God spurred the hearts of the pious people to action (110) and ended the cult of the evil demon by the overturning and shattering of Serapis*.[51]

No longer does Isis* wander in search of Osiris* through the

---

47. Tradition has it that Mark the Evangelist, under the direction of Peter, established the first church at Alexandria (Eusebius, *Historia Ecclesiastica* [Church History] II.16).
48. Apis was the sacred bull of Memphis worshipped by the ancient Egyptians. He is sometimes portrayed as a man with a bull's head.
49. Jupiter* was believed to have been buried at Cnossos on Crete. Fourth-century visitors were still shown his tomb (Firmicus Maternus, *De errore profanarum religionum* [On the Error of Pagan Religions] 7.6).
50. Diana was the Roman goddess identified with the Greek Artemis, the daughter of Zeus and Leto, whose temple at Ephesus was one of the wonders of the ancient world. Apollo*, the god of music, poetry and science and, among the Romans, of healing, was the brother of Diana. The apostle John settled in Ephesus and his tomb later became an object of great reverence among Christians. Pytho was a spirit or demon, apparently the one driven out by Paul at Ephesus (Acts 19.13).
51. The great temple of Serapis* at Alexandria, another wonder of the ancient world, was destroyed by a Christian mob with the support of imperial officials in 391 (A. Piganiol, *L'empire chrétien*, 2nd edn, Paris 1972, p. 285).

marshes of Pelusium with her bald-headed priests who beat their breasts, adding their own grief to one that does not concern them. And then, turning from their mad lamentation, they indulge in equally foolish joy, (115) pretending he is found by the same invention they used as they strayed looking for what they had never lost. How deep is the whirlpool of folly in which minds empty of God's light are drowned! Who, I ask, could be blinder than those who seek a man not even lost (120) and find him, although he does not exist anywhere to be found, while lamenting a grief entirely irrelevant to them? Choose your course, miserable folly. What do you worship — or weep for? The things you unite are incompatible; grief has no place with worship, yet you worship what you mourn and believe you should grieve for what you think divine. If they are gods, they are not sad; (125) or, if they are sad, they are not gods, but unhappy men. Condole with them, then, if they suffer the lot of men or venerate them as happy if gods; for it is clearly blind folly to worship the sad or mourn the blessed. So, is Isis* a goddess? Is any woman a goddess? (130) If a goddess, she has no body, and sex does not exist without a body nor birth without a sex. How, then, did she produce the Osiris* she is looking for? But a goddess can never be a mother or a mortal woman. For there is but one God, a threefold quality, one God the Father and (135) one Son with and within him and with him the Spirit of the Word, one with the Father: the three names are one God eternally. (140)

Carthage flourishes in power with her martyr Cyprian, from whom flowed streams of eloquence and blood to enrich the sands of thirsty Libya.[52] Not far from there Utica is made glorious by the white mass, (145) where her martyrs are gathered in a great heap of holy slaughter; one mound of blessed turf hiding many bodies rises high above the fields, bearing witness to men high in merit through the height of their grave. Thus Africa, fertile for Christ for many years, (150) multiplies its crops in abundance from so great a sowing and produces teachers outstanding in words and faith. No less favour was granted to the lands of the west. Ambrose gives glory to Italy, Vincent to Spain, Gaul boasts Martin as her patron and Aquitania Delphinus.[53] (155) Many other seeds of sanctity were scattered generously over those same shores in widely spread graves to bring light to the whole world by their heavenly virtues and cast out the primeval serpent all over the globe.

---

52. Cyprian was bishop of Carthage during the persecutions of Decius (249-51) and Valerian (253-60). His teachings on the church, its sacraments and the office of bishop proved formative in western theology.

53. Paulinus' western saints are a mixed group. Ambrose of Milan was an acquaintance and patron of Paulinus; Vincent of Saragossa was martyred during the persecutions of Diocletian; Martin of Tours was a controversial ascetic bishop who died in 397, the same year as Ambrose; Delphinus of Bordeaux was the bishop responsible for the conversion and baptism of Paulinus himself.

Another attack on the pagans is contained in the tenth poem of Prudentius' series of poems on martyrs. It differs from the rest in being much longer (1140 lines) and in not having a clear liturgical form. The subject is the passion and martyrdom of Romanus during the persecution by the emperor Galerius (306-11) for resisting attempts by the prefect, Asclepiades, to destroy the churches. Most of the poem consists of speeches made by Romanus justifying the Christian faith and attacking that of the pagans, with an interval describing the martyrdom of a child who has borne witness to the Trinity with amazing fluency and sophistication. The excerpted passage is the beginning of a speech by Romanus which is exceptionally miraculous because he has just had his tongue cut out. It supplies the only literary description of the pagan rite of the taurobolium*.[54]

---

Document 54: Prudentius, *Peristephanon* (Crowns of the Martyrs) X.1007-50

'Behold, I am here. The blood you see is truly mine, not that of a bull. Do you understand the blood I mean, most unhappy pagan, the sacred blood of your bull (1010) in whose ritualized slaughter you soak yourselves? Yes, in order to sanctify himself, the chief priest wears a peculiar band on his head, his temples bound with sacrificial fillets for the rite and, moreover, his hair fastened by a golden crown, (1015) in a silk robe belted in the Gabine fashion [round the waist] he is lowered into a trench dug deep underground. Over his head they construct a scaffold of criss-cross planking, leaving spaces open between the joints and then in many places they cut or bore through the surface and make a large number of holes in the wood with a sharp point (1020) so that many little openings are left visible. To this place an enormous bull with a fierce and shaggy forehead is led in procession hung with garlands of flowers across his shoulders or around his horns, while the victim's forehead gleams with gold (1025) and the shine of the plate reflects on his bristles. The brute beast to be sacrificed is placed in position and they tear open his chest with a consecrated hunting-spear. The wide wound spurts out a stream of hot blood which pours in a steaming flood onto the plank scaffolding below and (1030) spreads out in a wide and seething pool. Then it seeps in a shower through the numerous holes formed by the thousand gaps and drips down in a foul dew which the priest buried beneath welcomes, bowing his filthy head to take every drop, (1035) his clothes and his entire body made rotten. He even throws back his head, presents his cheeks to the stream, puts

---

54.   For the rite of the *taurobolium**: R. Duthoy, *The Taurobolium: Its Evolution and Terminology*, Leiden 1969.

his ears under it, his nose, his lips and bathes his very eyes in the flow. Nor does he spare his mouth but wets his tongue with it (1040) until the whole man has drunk in the dark blood. After the priests drag the stiffened carcass drained of blood off that scaffold the ghastly sight of the chief priest emerges and displays his wet soggy head, his clogged beard, his dripping fillet and blood-soaked vestments. They all greet this man contaminated with such defilement and filthy with the foulness of the victim just offered and they do him homage at a respectful distance, simply because the mere blood of a dead bull (1050) has washed him while he lay concealed in a disgusting hole underground.'

Among prose works containing anti-pagan polemic is that of Firmicus Maternus. Although better known for his work on astrology, Firmicus Maternus was also the author of an attack on oriental and Roman paganism and pagan mythology, the *De errore profanarum religionum* written in the 340s and dedicated to the emperors Constans and Constantius II. Although part of the text is lost, it provides important evidence for the conduct of the Mysteries and the formulae employed by the celebrants.[55]

Document 55: Firmicus Maternus, *De errore profanarum religionum* (On the Error of the Pagan Religions), 18, 21, 22

18. We may now explain the signs and symbols by which that pitiable gang of men recognize each other. For they have their own signs, and their own responses, which the Devil's teaching has entrusted to them in those assemblies of these sacrilegious men. In a certain temple, for a man to be allowed to enter to the innermost part he says, 'I have eaten from the timbrel, I have drunk from the cymbal, I have consigned the religious secrets to memory', which is rendered in Greek: 'I have eaten from the timbrel, I have drunk from the cymbal, I have become an initiate of Attis*'. Poor miserable man, to thus confess the crimes you have committed. You have drunk the death-bringing plague of poison, you have tasted the lethal cup with the touch of wicked madness. That food of yours is always followed by the penalty of death ... Far different is the food that generously offers salvation and life, far different the food that both commends and restores a man to the high God.

21. Let all the symbols of the profane religions be assembled in order so that we can demonstrate that the most evil Enemy of mankind has taken these from the holy and venerable oracles of

55. For details: C. Forbes' introduction to *Firmicus Maternus: The Error of the Pagan Religions*, New York 1970, pp. 1-41.

prophets to defile the wickedness of his own madness. For we find it said [in Greek], 'Hail, two-horned, two-formed one'. That god of yours is not two-formed but many-formed, for his dreadful appearance changes into many shapes.

22. We will adduce yet another symbol, that the wickedness of this corrupted way of thought may be revealed. We must describe the whole order of this thought so that all will agree that the law laid down by the divine power has been perverted by the crooked manipulation of the Devil. One night, an image is laid face upward on a couch and lamented with tears and rhythmic chants. Then, when they have glutted themselves with fake mourning, the light is brought in. The throats of all who have lamented are then anointed by the priest and, after the anointing, the priest whispers these words in a soft murmur [in Greek]: 'Take courage, initiates of a mystery of a god now saved. For you will come salvation from suffering.' Why do you encourage the wretched to rejoice? Why compel deceived people to be happy? What hope, what salvation do you promise with your deadly persuasions? Why do you incite them with a false promise?

Preserved among the works of St Augustine is a series of prose treatises now ascribed to the fourth-century author known as Ambrosiaster, whose real identity is unknown. His Chapter 114, *Adversum paganos* (Against the Pagans), contains arguments not commonly found elsewhere.[56]

Document 56: Ambrosiaster, *Quaestiones veteris et novi testamenti* (Questions on the Old and New Testaments) 114

1. I do not understand what justification the pagans can adduce for their daring to join battle with us or to make assaults upon our faith, seeing that they have no documentary proof of their allegations concerning their superstition, as I shall call it, rather than their religion. For they produce assertions of which they have no well-founded proof, as if it is they who should rather be regarded as the instigators and supporters of revolution. In the first place, they claim to worship gods, of whom they offer no visible sign or witness. They give the title of gods to personages who never ventured to claim it for themselves, with the result that man is regarded as the creator of gods, although God should be the creator of men: and, because of this, their claim is vain and empty. For whatever is without

56.  On the problems surrounding the identity and work of Ambrosiaster: P. de Labriolle, *The History and Literature of Christianity from Tertullian to Boethius*, London 1924, repr. 1968, pp. 288-90.

God cannot exist in a permanent form. That what I say is patently true is proved by their own writings, in which there is nothing said to be divine, nothing declared to be ordained at the command of God, but rather they claim that single individual men set up different kinds of sacrifice to divine powers for this or that reason, the establishment of which matched the deserts of their aim, as they were of a kind as to deserve nothing. Since, then, those whom they call gods gave no such instruction in their books, by what authority do pagans today act as they do or accept as done by others what is not confirmed by any mandate — although, even if a divine command could be proved, it should first be investigated whether these gods deserve or ought to be obeyed, although nowhere in history are there signs or prodigies to confirm their divine status?

2.   But being unable to stand up to these arguments, the pagans tend to take refuge with the elements, saying that they worship the powers that steer and guide the lives of men. Of these we may ask the same question as above, whether this is commanded or ordained by the God whom even they admit to be great and supreme, although they neglect him. For if this ought to be the case, an order should have come from him who is said to be their creator. If, however, there is no order of this kind, the worship is a presumption and invites punishment not reward, as it is an insult to the Creator that his slaves should be worshipped while the master is despised, that the emperor's ministers should be venerated while the emperor himself is scorned. How shall that crime of yours, punishable even in this life, not meet with severer penalties later?

3.   But perhaps, they may say that the command came from the elements themselves. Let them show us that instruction somewhere, let them read out that sometime they made some such utterance. For if they fail in this demonstration, what punishment is fit for people convicted of being the authors of a presumptuous and fictitious religion? The elements themselves are guiltless of this impiety. For the stars of the heavens themselves shall accuse them before God in judgement, as they prove their freedom of responsibility for this foolish course. Likewise too, those men whom the pagans claim as gods, although it is agreed that they were men, on first suffering torment for their sins shall turn their offence on the pagans' heads and, in their own defence, proclaim themselves guiltless as it was the pagans who first began to worship them as gods, although they had not ordered it so.

[Sections 4-5 describe how the Christian God has given sure proof of himself by direct speech, by the giving of the law and by testimonies of his goodness.]

6.   Therefore we practise nothing in the darkness, nothing in secret. For nothing known to be honourable is afraid to show itself in public: things shameful or dishonourable, on the other hand, modesty forbids to show their faces in the open. Therefore, the pagans

celebrate their mysteries in the dark, and wisely so. For they blush to perform them openly, as practices carried on thus in place of law tend to be revealed as shameful and those who call themselves wise should thus appear dull-witted to us whom they call fools.

[Sections 7-8 contrast effeminate eunuch priests with the chastity of Christians, and compare the religious law of pagans and Christians, and pagans' use of such words as 'wisdom' and 'chastity' to mean the opposite.]

9.   Let us now compare the content of the laws. The pagans admit even in their writings that they worship gods and goddesses; and what they say is true as they worship both male and female beings. For Janus* and Saturn*, Jupiter*, Mercury* and Apollo* and the rest, and likewise Minerva* and Isis* and that Frux [corn] and Venus* and the promiscuous Flora* and the rest are all gods and goddesses, as the histories of both Greeks and Romans tell us. But the Christians, poor souls, whom they call fools, worship only one god in their mystery, from whom come all things; nor do they worship anything created by him. For they know that he himself alone is enough for them and more than enough for their salvation, being well aware that they will offend him if they ascribe his glory and divinity to others, as no emperor allows his tribunes and counts to be worshipped in his name.

10.   Let the laws now be compared to see on which side lies wisdom, the one that worships the creator — or the created? The master — or the slave? It could happen that in some house some other man might be called master in addition to the first, just as the pagans, learned in legal matters, who seem so wise to themselves, worship many gods and goddesses in a world created by a single god. For they entitle governors and administrators of the world 'master' and 'god' and show their lack of forethought. To make an assertion that results in destruction is the mark of an improvident and foolish man, since God must, of necessity, visit punishment on those who allow their fellow-slaves to share the name of master and god.

11.   Then let our precepts be considered. Our law provides for the ordination of priests and ministers — whom they call stupid — who are holy men, free of sin and blameless; it is the pagan tradition on the contrary that their priests and ministers are not qualified unless they become women instead of men.

[Sections 11-12 provide further attacks on rites of Isis and others.]

13.   Their religious rites are also of this kind. Yet it was through the craftiness and wiles of Satan that later generations were ensnared by these inventions. Although these rites were not evolved without his connivance, yet he endowed certain aspects with a sort of auth-

ority, through which he might lure men into error, and it thus came about that falsehood was commended and a shameful fiction exonerated by their being handed down from antiquity. For through habit, what was actually shameful began to appear not to be so. When the honour of some was violated, at first they blushed: later, due to the soothing influence of habit, a sense of modesty, with altered appearance, retreated, especially if many were seen acting thus. For shameful things reap a quick profit when pagans said to be noble are seen to lose their honour; disgraced nobility easily finds imitators.

[Sections 14-23 provide further justification of Christian doctrine and refutation of the 'stupidity' of Christians.]

24. But the pagans maintain that they hold by the truth on grounds of antiquity because 'what is earlier', they say, 'cannot be false' — as if antiquity or long-established habit had a monopoly of judging the truth. Murderers or homosexuals or adulterers or other criminals could have produced a defence for their forbidden practices on this very ground, as they are ancient and began with the beginning of the world, whereas it is really from this fact that they should better understand the error of their ways, as what is culpable and shameful has clearly been bad from the first, while the honourable and sacred is deserving of worship: also that which was shameful and bad before cannot become holy and free of blame.

25. And, finally, the tradition of the pagans was undeniably the creation of man; but that our law was given by God is well attested. For on the mountain the majesty of God appeared, to give the law to men.

[Sections 25-30 provide biblical proofs of the power and effectiveness of God.]

31. Finally, those who today oppose him, tomorrow will justify their late knowledge of the truth by doing penance. For if our religion deserved hatred or contained any element of deceit, every day Christians would be becoming pagans; whereas in fact since this belief of ours is the truth, every day and every hour without a pause pagans, including philosophers and aristocrats who had maintained the fiction that Jupiter* is a god, now desert him and flee to take refuge with Christ, to whom is honour and glory, world without end.

# Chapter 5

# CHRISTIAN AND PAGAN ARISTOCRATS AT ROME

To assess the proper significance of the arguments and behaviour of Symmachus and Ambrose, and of pagans and Christians in general, they must be placed in the context of aristocratic society in Rome, and Milan, in the 380s and 390s. The two sides display a striking unanimity of background and culture, as well as (in most cases) a mutual respect and understanding not easily reconcilable with simple notions of a pagan/Christian 'conflict'.

Roman senatorial aristocrats, imbued with venerable traditions, derived their income from family estates scattered over Italy and much of the empire, and spent most of their time engaged in a life of cultured leisure in the congenial atmosphere of the Eternal City, punctuated, to a varying extent, by the holding of high administrative offices. The establishment of the court of the young Valentinian II at Milan (rather than at Trier, the capital of his father Valentinian I), not only brought the senators into even closer contact with the court but provided Christians with the opportunity of playing a prominent role in the official disestablishment of the old cults in the succeeding years.[1]

A further factor in this process of religious alignment is the traditional interplay between the public and private aspects of life and belief. The senators held the traditional priesthoods of Rome and fulfilled this public role by dedicating new temples and statues to the old gods. By the fourth century the more intimate salvation cults of the East — Mithras*, Great Mother* etc. — attracted their personal devotion and participation as well. This blending of the old and new, the public and the private, is reflected in several inscriptions dedicated to (or more frequently by) such aristocrats[2]

---

1. For details: J. Matthews, *Western Aristocracies and Imperial Court A.D. 364-425*, Oxford 1975, pp. 1-31, 183-222 and S. Dill, *Roman Society in the Last Century of the Western Empire*, London 1899, repr. 1958, pp. 3-26, 143-66.
2. The precise relationship between the traditional Roman and Oriental cults in the lives of the aristocracy remains a matter of debate. It used to be argued

and in the diatribes of their more passionate Christian critics.[3]
Besides these documents, it is the letters of Symmachus himself
that provide the most informative body of evidence for understanding the attitude of the pagan aristocracy to both the Christian
religion and their Christian antagonists. In these letters we see how
the distinction between pagan and Christian presented itself to a
leading Roman senator. We also catch some glimpse in them of
the role of religion in the public life of the senatorial aristocracy
and of how the sophisticated and mannered style of the correspondence and the social relationships it presupposes transcend the
pagan/Christian cleavage within senatorial society.[4] This helps us
to understand the remark of Prudentius that office-holding
remained a function of the aristocracy as a whole and was by no
means incompatible with the religious inclinations of the imperial
court.[5]

The Christianization of the aristocracy never replaced but was,
of necessity, accommodated to the prominent aspects of traditional
aristocratic behaviour.[6] Christian senators took a conspicuous role
in public religious ceremonial, as their pagan counterparts had
done, and retained their traditional avenues of patronage by, for
example, building churches.[7]

Much aristocratic time and attention was devoted to literary

that there was a strong distinction between the 'Roman' religion of someone
like Symmachus and the 'Oriental' preference of someone like Praetextatus
(D. Robinson, 'An Analysis of the Pagan Revival of the Late Fourth Century,
with especial reference to Symmachus', *Transactions of the American Philo-
logical Association*, 46, 1915, pp. 87-101, reflected in H. Bloch, 'A New Document of the Last Pagan Revival in the West, 393-394 A.D.', *Harvard
Theological Review*, 38, 1945, pp. 199-244 (with a useful table of priesthoods
held by individuals) and 'The Pagan Revival in the West at the End of the
Fourth Century' in A. Momigliano (ed.), *The Conflict between Paganism and
Christianity in the Fourth Century*, Oxford 1963, pp. 193-217). It is now clear,
however, that such a distinction is invalid and fails to take account of the
nature of the evidence, chiefly epigraphic, for the religious affiliations of aristocrats (J. Matthews, 'Symmachus and the Oriental Cults', *Journal of Roman
Studies*, 63, 1973, pp. 175-95).

3.   Documents 50 (p. 80), 51 (p. 84) and 52 (p. 86).
4.   J. Matthews, 'The Letters of Symmachus' in J. Binns (ed.), *Latin Literature
of the Fourth Century*, London 1974, p. 91.
5.   Document 47, p. 69.
6.   Matthews, *Western Aristocracies*, pp. 362-74. For attempts to 'rock the boat'
by senators, see P. Brown, 'The Patrons of Pelagius: the Roman Aristocracy
between East and West', *Journal of Theological Studies*, n.s. 21, 1970, pp.
56-72, reprinted in *Religion and Society in the Age of Saint Augustine*, London
1972, pp. 208-26.
7.   For a senatorial display of charity in St Peter's in Rome by the senator Pam-
machius, see Paulinus of Nola, *Epistula* (Letter) XIII.11ff.; for his churches:
Matthews, *Western Aristocracies*, p. 367.

activities — the production and patronage of poetry and oratory, the collection, editing and commentating on ancient texts. On the pagan side this emerges clearly in the letters of Symmachus and the poems of his friend Naucellius.[8] Symmachus himself claimed to be involved in editing 'the whole of the work of Livy' and Nicomachus Flavianus was renowned as a 'most erudite historian'.[9] From the perspective of a later generation, this flourishing group of pagan littérateurs suggested a tightly-knit literary circle, obsessed with the niceties of grammar and etymology. This was the 'age of Praetextatus' (*Saeculum Praetextati*), as recorded in the *Saturnalia* of Macrobius, c. 430,[10] a summary ideal of Roman culture before the final and decisive Christianization.

However, this way of life was common to both pagan and Christian aristocrats.[11] At Milan in the 380s Augustine had met Manlius Theodorus, a keen student of both early Greek philosophy and Neoplatonism, whose only extant work is a strictly classical one, *De metris* (On Metres).[12] In 395 Symmachus' friend, Sallust, was editing the *Metamorphoses* of Apuleius, a work on redemption through the mysteries of Isis, under the guidance of the Christian orator, Endelechius.[13] The continuity of classical culture is brought out, above all, in the subscriptions surviving in a text of Livy, which show three editors, Victorianus (Books I-X), Nicomachus Dexter (Books III-V) and, for Books VI-VIII, 'I, Nicomachus Flavianus, *vir clarissimus*, thrice Prefect of the City, edited [this book] at Enna'.[14] All these fifth-century editors continued the earlier literary

8.   F. Munari (ed.), *Epigrammata Bobiensia*, Rome 1955.

9.   For Symmachus' Livian enterprise: Symmachus, *Epistula* (Letter) IX.3 and for Nicomachus' historical reputation *CIL* VI.1782 (= Document 74, p. 112).

10.  For the dating of *Saturnalia*, a very significant point: Alan Cameron, 'The Date and Identity of Macrobius', *Journal of Roman Studies*, 56, 1966, pp. 25-38 (proposing c. 430) and J. Flamant, *Macrobe et le néoplatonisme latin à la fin du ive siècle*, Leiden 1977, p. 91 (suggesting 408-10).

11.  The common literary ground of pagan and Christian aristocrats is best illustrated by Alan Cameron, 'Paganism and Literature in Late Fourth Century Rome' in *Christianisme et Formes Littéraires de l'Antiquité tardive en occident (Fondation Hardt. Entretiens* t.XXIII), Geneva 1977, pp. 1-30. See also R. Markus, 'Paganism, Christianity and the Latin Classics' in Binns, *Latin Literature*, pp. 1-21.

12.  Augustine's acquaintance with Manlius is perhaps overrated (Matthews, *Western Aristocracies*, pp. 216-18).

13.  Endelechius was the official orator of the City of Rome in 395 and a Christian (ibid., pp. 250-1, with 'Severus Sanctus qui et Endelec(h)ius', *PLRE* II, p. 975).

14.  On this editorial activity: Cameron, 'Paganism and Literature', pp. 5-6, 26-7 and for the subscriptions themselves: O. Jahn, 'Uber die Subscriptionen in den Handschriften römischer Classiker', *Berichte der Sächsischen Gesellschaft der Wissenschaft*, 1851, pp. 327-72.

tradition, with one difference: they were all Christian. Victorianus, one of the editors of Livy, also edited the elder Nicomachus Flavianus' rendering of Philostratus' *Life* of Apollonius of Tyana, the pagan miracle-worker.[15]

Aurelius Symmachus is for several reasons the central figure among the pagan Roman aristocracy in the late fourth century. His eloquent plea for the restoration of the Altar of Victory attracted the admiration of all, even Christians. The publication of Symmachus' letters after his death ensured that posterity would be obliged to look at the late fourth-century Roman aristocracy through the eyes of Symmachus. In this chapter, therefore, it is expedient to group the documents relating to particular individuals in such a way that each individual, pagan and Christian, can be evaluated in terms of a single common denominator — Symmachus.

## (A) QUINTUS AURELIUS SYMMACHUS

The public career of Symmachus is summarized in the next document, an inscription dedicated to Symmachus by his son. He was *quaestor* and *praetor* before 365 when he was governor (*corrector*) of Lucania and Bruttium in South Italy. By 365 he was already *pontifex maior* and, as his letters show, took his religious duties seriously. In 369 and 370 he visited Valentinian I on the Rhine frontier in Gaul, and may then have received his title of 'Count of the Third Rank'. In 373 he was governor (*proconsul*) of Africa, and from summer 384 till early 385, just after the death of Praetextatus, was Prefect of the City, the office that he used to further the pagan representation on the Altar of Victory to the emperor. He rose to the height of *consul ordinarius* in 391 along with his fellow pagan, Tatian. In addition, he went on various embassies to the Imperial Court, as in 369 (to Valentinian I on the Rhine), 382 (Altar of Victory), and 387 (inauguration of consuls at Milan). Famous for his eloquence, he wrote not only the Letters and *Relationes*, but several speeches, including a thanks to the Senate for recalling his father who had been expelled from Rome by a mob for a reported injudicious remark, and panegyrics of the usurper Maximus (a source of some embarrassment) and Theodosius. His last letter dates from February 402 and he is assumed to have died soon after.[16]

15. For this work: P. Courcelle, *Late Latin Writers and Their Greek Sources*, Cambridge, Mass. 1969, pp. 189-90.
16. The best introductions to Symmachus are: Matthews, *Western Aristocracies*;

# (i) Inscription

> Document 57: *CIL* VI.1699 (=*ILS* 2946); Rome, Caelian Hill, home of the Symmachi
>
> To Q(uintus) Aur(elius) Symmachus, v(ir) c(*larissimus*), quaest(or), praet(or), higher pontiff (*pontifex maior*), governor (*corrector*) of Lucania and Bruttium, Count of the Third Order, proconsul of Africa, Prefect of the City, *consul ordinarius*, most eloquent orator, Q(uintus) Fab(ius) Memm(ius) Symmachus, v(ir) c(*larissimus*) to the best of fathers.

# (ii) Letters of Symmachus

> Document 58: IX.108 (to a Vestal virgin, date unknown)
>
> All things that are discussed on no good authority are uncertain, but I have no time for gossip involving the reputation of a holy virgin. Whereupon, with the duty of a priest and the oath of a senator, I am advised to make known what I have found out. You are said to wish to give up the mystery of the Vestals* before the statutory number of years has lapsed. I do not yet believe in the rumour but I await a statement from your lips either to admit or reject the doubt which derives from [unconfirmed] opinion.

> Document 59: IX.147 (to an anonymous magistrate, date unknown)
>
> In the tradition and manner of our forefathers the investigation of our college has apprehended the fornication of Primigenia, long since a Vestal* priestess at Alba. The reports show that the act was made clear in the confessions both of she who despoiled her chastity and of Maximus with whom she committed the despicable crime. It remains that the severity of the laws be visited on those who have polluted the public ceremonies by such shameful wickedness, which

*Footnote 16 continued*
   Dill, *Roman Society*, pp. 143-66; J. McGeachy, *Quintus Aurelius Symmachus and the Senatorial Aristocracy of the West*, Diss., Chicago 1942; R. Klein, *Symmachus. Eine tragische Gestalt des ausgehenden Heidentums*, Darmstadt 1971. The most detailed study of Symmachus' writings remains the introduction to the edition of his works by O. Seeck, *Q. Aurelii Symmachi quae supersunt* (*MGH AA* VI), Berlin 1883, repr. 1961. For full references for his public career: 'Q. Aurelius Symmachus 4', *PLRE* I, pp. 865-70.

action is reserved for you in accordance with the most recent precedent. You will therefore be good enough, with regard to the common good and the laws, to punish suitably a crime that has been the one most seriously avenged by all eras up to the present. Farewell.

## Document 60: IX.148 (to an anonymous magistrate, date unknown)

In accordance with the most recent precedent, the punishment of the virgin Primigenia who used to tend the shrine at Alba is entrusted by our college to our most distinguished and excellent brother, the Prefect of the City. However, in view of the reasonable grounds set out in his letter — he points out that it is not lawful for someone accused of such a great crime to enter inside the walls of the eternal city nor can he himself come out to remote parts, since a crime must be atoned for where it is committed — we have considered it necessary to invoke the neighbouring power, namely he who has charge over the provincial jurisdiction, so that to Primigenia who dishonoured the secrets of the chaste godhead and her corrupter Maximus, who did not in fact deny the shame, may be extended the severity that is always visited upon these crimes. Be so good therefore as to review these confessions which betray the tragedy of an unspeakable crime, and to revenge the injury to a most chaste era by punishment of the accused.

## Document 61: I.64 (380)

Symmachus to his brother, Celsinus Titianus[17]

1. Perhaps you will be surprised that I am recommending a bishop. His cause compels me to do it not his sect. For Clement, while discharging the duty of a good man, protected his home-town, Caesarea, winning the favour of our very great princes.[18] You have heard it said that in the barbarian rebellion all the gold and silver in Mauretania, private and public, sacred and profane, has been consumed by the destruction of the enemy.[19]

17. Titianus was Vicar of Africa in 380, the year of his death. He was also a priest of Vesta* and the Sun. See further: 'Celsinus Titianus 5', *PLRE* I, pp. 917-18.
18. i.e. the emperors Gratian and Theodosius.
19. This refers to the Moors' revolt led by Firmus in 373 when the elder Theodosius, the emperor's father, was sent against them. For Symmachus' personal interest in Caesarea: J. Matthews, 'Symmachus and the *magister militum* Theodosius', *Historia*, 20, 1971, pp. 126-7.

2.   It happened at that time that even the deposit in the treasury was snatched away by the law of war. This the right of the treasury demanded back from the nobles of the city who were still alive because they had fled. It would have been a wretched and harsh situation, if the diligence of Clement had not put the justice of our times into action. I would say that he contributed to the reputation of our age no less than to the safety of the citizens. For what, besides envy, will the treasury get in return if wealth is demanded from an impoverished local senate? You know the sequence of events. It remains for you to strive to make the favouring wind of your prayer fill the sails of its fulfilment. Farewell.

## (B) VETTIUS AGORIUS PRAETEXTATUS AND FABIA ACONIA PAULINA

Vettius Agorius Praetextatus,[20] in an illustrious public career, was quaestor, praetor, governor (*corrector*) of Tuscia and Umbria (central Italy) and governor (*consularis*) of Lusitania in Spain before 362, when he was made proconsul of Achaea by Julian. While still in office in 364 he successfully interceded with Valentinian I for the preservation of the Mysteries. As Prefect of the City in 367-8, he dealt with the riots attendant on the rivalry of Damasus and Ursinus for the papal chair, by expelling the latter, and introduced other reforms. He was ambassador from the senate in 370 and perhaps on other occasions, and his career culminated in 384 when he was Praetorian Prefect of Illyricum and consul designate. His numerous priesthoods are listed on an inscription (Document 65). His view of worldly Christians is summarized in his famous remark to Pope Damasus: 'Make me Bishop of Rome and I'll become a Christian overnight!'[21]

His wife, Fabia Aconia Paulina, was the daughter of the distinguished Aconius Catullinus (see Document 20) and herself the holder of several priesthoods.

### (i) Inscriptions

Document 62: *CIL* VI.102 (= *ILS* 4003); Rome, on the architrave of a portico on the slope of the Capitoline Hill, 367-8

Vettius Praetextatus, *v(ir)* c(*larissimus*), Prefect of the City

---

20.   For Praetextatus: 'Vettius Agorius Praetextatus 1', *PLRE* I, pp. 722-4.
21.   Jerome, *Contra Iohannem Ierosolymitanum* (Against John of Jerusalem), 8.

replaced the holy images of the D[ei C]onsentes[22] together with the adornment of the whole area and restored the cult to its ancient form. The curator of the work was Longeius, v(ir) c(larissimus), consular [of the public works?].

---

Document 63: CIL VI.1777 (= ILS 1258); Rome, Aventine Hill

To Vettius Agorius Praetextatus, v(ir) c(larissimus) and ill(ustris) governor (corrector) of the province of Tuscia and Umbria, governor (consularis) of Lusitania, proconsul of Achaea, Prefect of the City, Praetorian Prefect of Illyricum, Italy and Africa, consul designate, seven times ambassador of the most esteemed order (the senate), and always prominent in the accomplishment of difficult pleas, deserving of honour as a parent both privately and publicly. The setting up of decorations and their placement so that the abode of his statue should be honoured were supervised by ... [the name is missing].

---

Document 64: CIL VI.1778; Rome, Caelian Hill, 387

To Vettius Agorius Praetextatus, v(ir) c(larissimus), priest of Vesta*, priest of the Sun, quindecemvir, augur, initiate of the taurobolium*, curial, temple overseer (neocorus), high priest (hierophanta), father of the sacred objects − quaestor designate, urban praetor, governor (corrector) of Tuscia and Umbria, governor (consularis) of Lusitania, proconsul of Achaea, Prefect of the City, twice[23] Praetorian Prefect of Italy and Illyricum, consul designate. Dedicated on February 1st, in the third consulship of our Lord Flavius Valentinian and of Eutropius.

---

Document 65: CIL VI.1780 (= ILS 1260); Rome

To Fabia Aconia Paulina, c(larissima) f(emina), daughter of Aconius Catullinus, v(ir) c(larissimus),[24] formerly Prefect and consul ordinarius. Wife of Vettius Praetextatus, v(ir) c(larissimus), Prefect and consul designate, consecrated at Eleusis to the gods Iacchus*,

---

22. The Dei Consentes were the Roman version of the Athenian twelve gods − six male, six female. Originally gilt statues of them stood in the forum. This porticus was built to house them later.
23. This is a mistake on the part of the stone-cutter. Praetextatus was Praetorian Prefect only once (384).
24. For Catullinus see Document 20, p. 19.

Ceres* and Cora*; consecrated at Laerna to the gods Liber*, Ceres* and Cora*, consecrated to the goddesses at Aegina; initiate of the taurobolium*, of Isis*, high priestess (*hierophantria*) of the Greek goddess Hecate*, of the sacred goddess Ceres.

## Document 66: CIL VI.2145 (= ILS 1161); Rome, Esquiline Hill

To Coelia Concordia, chief of the Vestal Virgins. Fabia Paulina, c(*larissima*) f(*emina*), arranged to have this statue built and put in position, because of her [Coelia's] scrupulous modesty and outstanding piety towards the divine ritual and because she had previously put up a statue[25] to her [Paulina's] husband Vettius Agorius Praetextatus, v(*ir*) c(*larissimus*), outstanding in every way and worthy to be worshipped by the virgins and priests of that order.

## Document 67: CIL VI.1779 (=ILS 1259); Rome, date uncertain

[Funeral monument of Praetextatus and Paulina now in the Capitoline Museum, Rome.]

On The Front:

To the Divine Shades. Vettius Agorius Praetextatus, augur, priest of Vesta*, priest of the Sun, *quindecemvir*, curial of Hercules, consecrated to Liber* and the Eleusinian mysteries*, high priest, temple overseer (*neocorus*), initiate of the taurobolium*, Father of the Fathers [priest of Mithras*]; but in public office: quaestor designate, urban praetor, governor (*corrector*) of Tuscia and Umbria, governor (*consularis*) of Lusitania, proconsul of Achaea, Prefect of the City, seven times sent by the senate as ambassador, twice Praetorian Prefect of Italy and Illyricum, designated *consul ordinarius*, and Aconia Fabia Paulina c(*larissima*) f(*emina*), consecrated to Ceres* and the Eleusinian mysteries*, consecrated at Aegina to Hecate*, initiate of the taurobolium*, high priestess.
These two lived together for forty years.

On The Right:

Vettius Agorius Praetextatus to his wife Paulina. Paulina, associate of truth and chastity, dedicated in temples and friend of the div-

---

25.  For a senatorial request for a statue to Praetextatus see Symmachus, *Relationes* (State Papers) XII and for Symmachus' attitude to the Vestals' proposal see his *Epistula* (Letter) II.36 (= Document 77, p. 113).

ine powers, putting her husband before herself, Rome before her man, modest, faithful, pure in mind and body, kind to all, a blessing to her household.

## On The Left:

Vettius Agorius Praetextatus to his wife Paulina. Paulina partner of my heart, nurse of modesty, bond of chastity, pure love and loyalty produced in heaven, to whom I have entrusted the deep hidden secrets of my heart, gift of the gods who bind our marriage couch with friendly and modest ties; by the devotion of a mother, the gratitude of a wife, the bond of a sister, the modesty of a daughter, and by all the loyalty friends show we are united by the custom of age, the pact of consecration, by the yoke of the marriage vow and perfect harmony, helpmate of your husband, loving, adoring, devoted.

## On The Back:

[Paulina to Praetextatus] The glory of my parents gave me nothing greater than to have seemed already worthy of my husband; but all light and glory is my husband's name. Agorius, sprung of proud lineage, you illumine your country, the senate and your wife by your integrity of mind, your character and your scholarship all at once. By these you attained the highest peak of virtue, for by translating whatever is proclaimed in either tongue by the thought of the wise, to whom the gate of heaven lies open, both the poems which the learned have composed and the prose works recited aloud, you have improved upon what you have found written down. Yet these things are of little account. You, a holy man, and priest of the mysteries, conceal in the secret places of your heart what you discovered in the sacred initiations and with your manifold learning you worship the divine power, uniting with your kindness your wife as your associate with the sacred objects, confidante of men and gods, and in one mind with you as she was. What may I now say of the offices and powers, joys sought by men in their prayers, which you who regard yourself as a priest of the gods and are marked out by your priestly headbands, always consider transient and trivial? You, O husband, deliver me pure and chaste from the lot of death by the goodness of your teaching, lead me into the temples and dedicate me to the gods as their handmaid. With you as witness I am initiated into all the mysteries. You, in your duty as husband, consecrate me as priestess of Didymenes [Cybele*] and Attis* through the rites of the bull. You instruct me, as a priestess of Hecate, in the threefold secrets and you prepare me for being worthy of the rites of Greek Ceres*. Because of you everyone proclaims me holy and blessed, since it is you who spread my goodness throughout the world. Although unknown I am known to all. With you as my husband how could I fail to please? The matrons of Romulus' city seek me as a model and regard their offspring as beautiful if it resembles yours. Men and women alike both seek after

and acclaim the honours which you, my teacher, have given me.
Now, robbed of all this I, your grief-stricken wife, am wasting away.
Happy would I have been had the gods granted that my husband
had outlived me. Yet I am happy because I am yours, was yours
and soon shall be yours after death.[26]

# (ii) Letters of Symmachus

## Document 68: 1.46 (before 381)

Symmachus to Agorius Praetextatus
    1.  I have been able to be brief as I think my brother [Titianus]
will give you fuller satisfaction with his conversation than will my
letter, but honourable discharge of obligation must be regarded as
of more profit than wordless inactivity. So there is no need for silence
in order that the esteem of friendship be brought to me the recipient.
Nor, so that something is left for the bearer to tell, should everything
be committed to a letter. Note, however, the chief points of the
news and the main matters of business which my brother is
instructed to expand on when requested.
    2.  It has been agreed among the state priests that we should
entrust the care of the gods to the guardianship of the citizens for
public worship. In fact the favour of the heavens is forfeited if it
is not upheld by ritual. Therefore, much more distinction has been
given to the heavenly honour than was the case. I suppose you are
waiting to hear everything else from me. My dear Titianus, to whom
I have delegated the task of explaining more liberally what you wish,
will provide the information. If you have not already received word
of the imperial edict, he will explain it to you, as an expert. You
have recovered your statues with almost the same popular accla-
mations with which you lost them. You laugh? You may well laugh.
You can only laugh because you were not there. I say no more lest
I who have briefly passed over the good news should appear to
linger over unsavoury things. Farewell.

---

26.  Praetextatus' death gave rise to considerable mourning at Rome. Symmachus
    told the emperor in Milan: 'I am compelled by the necessity of my public duty
    not to hold my peace on the death of an illustrious man, although my grief
    is still fresh. Vettius Praetextatus, a man the equal of the men of old, endowed
    with every virtue, whose distinction was outstanding, the fates have snatched
    away to the great grief of his country' (*Relationes* |State Papers| XI). Jerome,
    on the other hand, was keen to point out that 'he now lies forsaken and naked,
    not in a shining white palace in heaven as his unfortunate widow falsely
    declares, but in the filthy darkness of hell' (*Epistula* |Letter| XXIII.3).

## Document 69: I.47 (about 383)

Symmachus to Agorius Praetextatus
1.    The reasons for our mutual silence are different but the result is the same. Attention to priestly duties has prevented me; the indifference of leisure at Baiae you. For a relaxed mind makes a man no less idle than a busy one. Nor is it remarkable if that bay claims you entirely for itself since it is on sound authority that Hannibal himself, unconquered in war, surrendered to Campania. The lotus tree which kept back strangers from their journey and the persuasive potions of Circe and the trio of winged maidens [Sirens] could not match the allurement of its earth and sky.[27]
2.    Nor do I assert that you spend decadent holidays or think that your virtue is dulled by pleasures. But as long as you read for yourself, write for yourself and, in your weariness of city affairs, subdue your great mind in solitude, you will totally fail to carry out the duties of friendship. Why do you not take up your pen and respond with a like courtesy to the esteem in which I hold you? Unless you prefer to undertake the authority of the pontiff many resolutions need to be passed by us in the college. Who granted you this cessation of public duty? You will experience the jurisdiction of the priest if you do not satisfy the jurisdiction of a friend. Farewell.

## Document 70: 1.48 (before 385)

Symmachus to Agorius Praetextatus
Benevolent gods! How nothing is safe and certain for mankind! No doubt you have retired to Baiae to ease your mind. What evil eye has been cast on your intended repose? Has the health of Paulina therefore, our shared concern, reached a crisis or is your fear for her so great that you consider all her inconveniences take on the form of danger? Whichever of these it is, you should bear in mind the painful days and watchful nights you have passed. We are born doomed to endure frequent tribulation. Pleasures are fleeting and the enjoyment of every good is as brief as the experience is superficial. However, let these things be left to the arguments of philosophers. Let us now encourage our minds to a more joyful disposition when the peace of the gods has once again placed the health of our Paulina on a solid footing.

---

27.   For these Homeric allusions: *Odyssey* IX.91; X.316; XIII.39-57.

## Document 71: I.49 (about 378)

Symmachus to Agorius Praetextatus
      You ask, as a citizen born for the public good, what is the news about these worrying matters that is closest to the truth. We have learnt about our good fortune from reliable sources;[28] but later the suspicion born of a long silence has provided room for anxious rumours. But I do not bother myself with such opinions which come forward on no authority. I am greatly vexed in my mind that despite the multiple sacrifices often repeated through each of the powers, the prodigy of Spoleto is not yet atoned for in the public name. For the eighth victim scarcely appeased Jupiter* and the eleventh gift was made unsuccessfully to the public Fortune with many cattle as victims. You realize what our position is. Now that it is my purpose to call my colleagues into session, I will see that you are informed if the divine remedies accomplish anything. Farewell.

## Document 72: I.50 (before 377)

Symmachus to Agorius Praetextatus
      1.   Secure in the fact of your friendship, I take it in a fair and good spirit if I am wronged in any way by one who is fond of me; but negligence of duty is unbecoming to your character, which lacks nothing praiseworthy. You think that I am complaining because you write nothing and make ready to refute this charge because you do recall having written something. Actually I would be only slightly hurt if you were silent compared with this fact: that you sent to my father and myself a single letter, and an exceptionally brief one at that. So do we not both seem to you to be worth a separate page?
      2.   You will say that it was an honour for me to be associated with my parent. There are other things that I wish to share or have in common with him. Love should be conveyed to me personally. Therefore do away with letters that sound like an edict. Abandon all scorn from which this attention to brevity derived. But I must be very careful about going on at length lest the prolixity of my complaint be more annoying to you than the brevity of your letter to me. It remains for me to beg the gods that you might, as soon as possible, visit us again in the fullness of joy. It will be easy to redeem the brevity of your writing with lengthy conversation. Farewell.

28.   Seeck (*Q. Aurelii Symmachi*, p. lxxxix) considers this a reference to Sebastianus' victory over the Goths (Ammianus XXXI.11.4). The 'reliable source' may be Sebastianus' own exaggerated account (Ammianus XXXI.11.12).

Document 73: I.51 (383)

Symmachus to Agorius Praetextatus
We had decided to stay away outside the city still[29] but word of our weakening fatherland has changed my intentions since, with everybody facing hardship, my own safety seemed to pale into insignificance. Moreover the management of the holy priesthood that I hold requires of me both attention and the fulfilment of my duties in the appointed month. Nor does my conscience allow me to be replaced by a colleague when there is so much negligence among the priests. In other times it was a simple thing to substitute in divine ritual; now being absent from the altars is a form of self-advancement for Romans. How long will Etruria detain you? We are already complaining of there being something important for it to be preferred to your fellow citizens for so long. Although staying in the country is more pleasant, you cannot enjoy rest properly if you are anxious for absent friends. Farewell.

## (C) NICOMACHUS FLAVIANUS

Having held a quaestorship and praetorship, Virius Nicomachus Flavianus became governor (*consularis*) of Sicily in 364-5, the year of the elder Symmachus' prefecture of the city of Rome. In 377 he was Vicar of Africa and in 389-90 Quaestor of the Sacred Palace, a key financial post, under Valentinian II. In 390 he became Praetorian Prefect of Italy and Illyricum but, on the death of Valentinian II, was replaced in Illyricum by a nominee of Theodosius, Apodemius. In spring 393, Flavianus joined Eugenius on his entry into Italy and was reappointed Praetorian Prefect by the usurper. In 394, he was consul (without a colleague) down to his suicide after the defeat of Eugenius in September of that year.

His son, Nicomachus Flavianus, the editor of Livy, was governor (*consularis*) of Campania, proconsul of Asia in 382-3, and Prefect of the City for the first time under Eugenius, an office later not officially recognized, and twice more under Honorius in 399-400 and 408. In 431 he was Praetorian Prefect of Italy, Illyricum and Africa; his holding of office coincided with the publication of Macrobius' *Saturnalia* and rehabilitation of the memory of the elder Nicomachus.[30]

---

29. We prefer to read *adhuc* (Seeck) and see no reason to adopt *ad K.Oct*, the reading of Callu (*Symmaque, Lettres* [Budé], Paris 1972, p. 113) which has no manuscript support.
30. For the career of father and son: 'Virius Nicomachus Flavianus 15', *PLRE*

# (i) Inscription

---

### Document 74: *CIL* VI.1782 ( = *ILS* 2947); Rome, 394

Quintus Fab(ius) Memmius Symmachus, *v*(*ir*) *c*(*larissimus*) to his
most excellent father-in-law Virius Nicomachus Flavianus, *v*(*ir*)
*c*(*larissimus*), quaestor, praetor, higher pontiff (*pontifex maior*),
governor (*consularis*) of Sicily, Vicar of Africa, quaestor in the
imperial palace, twice Praetorian Prefect, *consul ordinarius*, most
erudite historian.

---

# (ii) Letters of Symmachus

---

### Document 75: II.7 (383-4)

Symmachus to his brother Flavianus
1.   At this time I would consider you particularly fortunate that,
sheltered from the inconveniences being suffered by our fatherland,
you are at leisure, if I did not know that good citizens and those
like you bear more heavily the adversities that they do not see. It
is in the nature of things in fact that whatever is learned from another
appears harsher and more serious. Moreover a faultless spirit thinks
that its uprightness is diminished if it is absent from the dangers
of its friends.
2.   I am saying this, not to encourage your prompt return but
to let you know that there is nothing in the tribulations we share
to cause you to hasten it. How could you aid the public anxiety,
although you are the most sensible of men, if you were to return?
In the first instance there is no room for offering advice; opinions
are weighed according to the character of those expressing them.
When does one resist a superior? When does one give ground to
an equal? From now on the present situation does not require wisdom but good fortune.
3.   We fear a failure in the corn supply even though all those
whom Rome has supported with a bare and full breast have been
expelled from the city.[31] We may well find healing by these remedies,
but how great a hatred against us among the provincials does this

---

*Footnote 30 continued*
I, pp. 347-9 and 'Nicomachus Flavianus 14', *PLRE* I, pp. 345-7. On the elder
Flavianus see J. O'Donnell, 'The Career of Virius Nicomachus Flavianus',
*Phoenix*, 32, 1978, pp. 129-43.

31.  Symmachus' worry over a corn shortage at Rome in 384 is evident from *Relationes* (State Papers) IX, XVIII, XXXV, XXXVII. Ammianus (XIV.6.19)
complained that, although foreigners like himself were expelled from Rome
in 384, foreign dancing girls were allowed to stay.

security arouse? Gods of the fatherland pardon our neglect of sacred things! Banish this dreadful famine! May our city recall as soon as possible those whom it reluctantly sent away. I do not like to speak with you more than is necessary about the misfortunes we share. Take care of your health and whatever is beyond the power of human beings entrust to the protection of the gods.

---

## Document 76: II.34 (before 390)

Symmachus to his brother Flavianus

1. I was thinking that, with the festival of the Mother of the gods approaching, you might be getting ready to return. You advance your journey to Daunii and leave us and your country behind you. Ridicule as you wish the complaisance of those friends who, if annoyed by your wronging them like this, would in retaliation at least refrain from writing. But now we soften your departure by our duties and apply soothing balms to your mind, though you put attention to domestic affairs before everything.

2. For remember that you have decorated your letter with this preamble: that nothing at this time should be treated more seriously than domestic affairs. When I think about the strength of your character, I know this was conceived as a joke. For when has the loftiness of your mind been distracted by rather paltry anxieties? I consider, therefore, that you are contemplating offering words to others who are not admitted to the sanctuary of your mind. There is only one way you will satisfy me — by ceasing your letters of defence and returning home in person.

---

## Document 77: II.36 (385)

Symmachus to his brother Flavianus

1. Is our common parent [Rome] really so pleased that it is necessary for you to stay away longer than I would wish? Or do you avoid city affairs so much that you disappoint my expectation by a pious excuse? And certainly nothing that a good soul and sincere nature could embrace is done or said here. But however these things are, if you were at Rome perhaps they would diminish with our mutual assistance. For the moment, since I am alone, I endure the more weighty misfortunes of affairs. Accept this one matter as an example from which you can surmise the rest.

2. The virgins, priestesses of sacred Vesta*, propose dedicating a personal statue to our beloved Praetextatus. The priests were consulted and, without taking into account reverence for the high priesthood, long established practice and the current situation (except for the few who agreed with me), agreed to erect his image.

3. I would remark that such homage to men does not become

the honourable position of the virgins nor does it accord with tradition, as the founder of our religious rites, Numa*, their preserver Metellus and all the chief priests were never previously accorded it. Yet I keep quiet about these things lest they be reported to the rivals of our cult and provide a scandal for those whose opinions are not in accordance with tradition. I merely put it on record that one should avoid a precedent lest something which derived from a just beginning should soon, by improper influence, come into the hands of the unworthy.

4.  So as not to go on too long I enclose my actual speech which, although it had the approval of respectable people, was perhaps refuted by numbers, although in pontifical decisions the procedure is not the same as in the senate. But ignorance of this will make it of little account. If you had been present at this session the good sense of both of us would have achieved much. Whereupon, as soon as our common parent [i.e. Rome] emerges from the uncertainty of her illness, restore yourself to me, so that our shared consolations may make the course of our life more smooth.

---

## Document 78: II.50 (before 390)

Symmachus to his brother Flavianus
      You already know that we will set out on a journey home with the favour of the gods. But duty counselled that you be informed about the date too. Therefore learn that tomorrow we are to take the road once again and because you are most careful about keeping promises remember to devote your attention to the public ceremony.

---

## Document 79: II.53 (before 390)

Symmachus to his brother Flavianus
      You perform the duty of a good brother, but give up reminding one already mindful of it. The ceremonies of the gods and the prescribed feasts of the divine beings are known to us. Unless by chance you demand that I alone take on your turn in the rites and, as is customary for the divine cult to demand, you put your obligations onto me. Enjoy an abundance of luxuries; we will take care of responsibilities. But remember when your holidays are over to make participants in your luxury those whom you strove so hard to have as fasting companions.[32]

---

32.  This apparently refers to the annual fast held in honour of Ceres on 4 October (Robinson, 'An Analysis of the Pagan Revival', p. 95).

Document 80: II.59 (393)

Symmachus to his brother Flavianus
    1.  I was at my suburban estate which borders on the Appian
Way when the messenger sent for the purpose delivered your letter
to me. You know the area we are talking about, where I have put
up a large house within narrow limits. We have spent a short while
here in delightful ease — if any ease is delightful without you. Now,
because of the Vestal holiday I am hurrying home uncertain whether
I will remain within the city or return to the outskirts again.
    2.  Since you have certainly been away longer than is reason-
able I must know what you are deciding to do. For the designation
of my [son as a] candidate summons you into our assembly, with
the support of the gods, as soon as possible. You will adorn it above
all those who attend us whether with the duties of kinship or friendship.

## (D) SEXTUS PETRONIUS PROBUS AND ANICIA FALTONIA PROBA

The greatest of all senatorial office-holders, Sextus Claudius
Petronius Probus, was described by Ammianus as 'a fish out of
water' when not holding office. After holding the quaestorship and
urban praetorship, he was proconsul of Africa in 358, and then
embarked on a series of Praetorian prefectures, holding that of
Illyricum in 364, Gaul in 365 and Illyricum, Italy and Africa in
368-75. In 371, while at Sirmium, he considered running away
from an invasion of Sarmatians and Quadi, but later thought better
of it; he was *consul posterior* (lesser consul) in the same year. In
383 he was again Praetorian Prefect of Illyricum, Italy and Africa,
and till his death sometime after 388 remained loyal to Valentinian
II. He married into the Anicii and his two sons were consuls
together in 395, and recipients of a panegyric by Claudian on the
'glorious offspring of Probus' (*clara pignora Probi*).[33]

### (i) Inscriptions

Document 81: *CIL* VI.1751 ( = *ILS* 1268); Rome, Pincian Hill,
    378

    To Petronius Probus, *v(ir) c(larissimus)*, chief of the nobility, light

33.  On Probus himself : 'Sextus Claudius Petronius Probus 5', *PLRE* I, pp. 736-40;

of letters and eloquence, model of authority, master of foresight and management, fountain of philanthropy, advocate of moderation, chief priest of devotion; proconsul of Africa, Praetorian Prefect of Illyricum, Italy and Africa, *consul ordinarius*. His tenants in Venetia and Histria [dedicate this] to their most outstanding patron on account of the extraordinary kinds of relief [shown] towards them. Dedicated on August 8th in the sixth consulship of our Lord Valens Augustus and the second of our Lord Valentinian Augustus.

## Document 82: *CIL* VI.1753 (= *ILS* 1267); Rome

To Sextus Petronius Probus, chief of the Anician household, proconsul of Africa, Praetorian Prefect four times of Italy, Illyricum, Africa and Gaul, *consul ordinarius*, father of consuls. His most devoted children Anicius Hermogenianus Olybrius, *v(ir)* c(*larissimus*), *consul ordinarius*, and his wife Anicia Juliana, c(*larissima*) f(*emina*) dedicated [this].

## Document 83: *CIL* VI.1755; Rome

To Anicia Faltonia Proba, trustee of the ancient nobility, pride of the Anician family, a model of the preservation and teaching of chastity, descendant of consuls, mother of consuls; her most loyal children Anicius Hermogenianus Olybrius, *v(ir)* c(*larissimus*), *consul ordinarius* and his wife Anicia Juliana, c(*larissima*) f(*emina*) dedicated this.

## Document 84: *CIL* VI.1754 (= *ILS* 1269); Rome, atrium of Domus Caesiana

To Anicia Faltonia Proba, adornment of the Amnii, Pincii and Anicii, wife of a consul, daughter of a consul, mother of consuls; Anicius Probinus, *v(ir)* c(*larissimus*), *consul ordinarius*, and Anicius Probus, *v(ir)* c(*larissimus*), *quaestor candidatus*, her sons, beholden, dedicated this to her maternal merits.

*Footnote 33 continued*
and on Proba: 'Anicia Faltonia Proba 3', *PLRE* I, pp. 732-3. For the sons: Anicius Hermogenianus Olybrius 2', *PLRE* I, pp. 630-40 and 'Anicius Probinus I', *PLRE* I, pp. 734-5. Claudian's panegyric is discussed by Alan Cameron, *Claudian. Poetry and Propaganda at the Court of Honorius*, Oxford 1970, pp. 30-6.

Document 85: *CIL* VI.1756; epitaph of Probus from his mausoleum, St Peter's, Rome

(a)   Stripped of your garment [of mortality] you safely run your course over the expanse of the heavens untouched by vice; like your name in probity your fame resounds in your character too; washed clean in the Jordan you are now Probus [i.e. upright] better than before. (5) Rich in wealth, of noble family, exalted in office and distinguished in your Consulship, worthy of your consular grandfather, twice governing the people in your twofold prefecture – these worldly trappings, these noble titles you rose above in age through the gift granted you by Christ. (10) This is your true office, this your nobility. Previously you rejoiced in the honour of the royal table, in the emperor's ear and the friendship of royalty. Now, closer to Christ after attaining the abode of the saints, you enjoy a new light. Christ is present as your light. (15) O Probus never be mourned for by your own kin! While you were alive and the breath of life governed these limbs of yours, you were foremost and second to none of the senators in virtue. Now, renewed, you have eternal rest and you wear gleaming white garments darkened by no stain, and (20) are a new dweller in unaccustomed mansions. With these thoughts console your people O Christ, although grace, your grace, does not seek the comforts of grief. He lives in the eternal abode of paradise in blessedness who, as he passed from view, (25) put on the new garments of his heavenly duty. When he passed on, Belial retired and groaned that nothing here was his. May you, Christ, I pray, join him to the heavenly choirs, let him hymn you and look on you forever, and ever beloved may he hang upon your word, bringing aid to his children and his wife.

(b)   Whoever you are who marvel at the lofty heights of this tomb, you will say – 'How great was the Probus who lies here!' Greater than his consular forebears and his wife's ancestors, and greater than a [normal] consul because he himself as consul restored two consular households, (5) four times Prefect beloved throughout the world, but having surpassed in reputation every mortal in the world. Alas, Rome, he who would demand for you eternal years, why did he not live to match his prayers for your well-being? For, when a month stayed his sixty years, (10) he was snatched from the embrace of his beloved Proba to heaven. But far be it from you, Rome, to believe that your Probus should have died for such services as his; he lives and possesses the stars; friend of virtue, faith, duty and honour; not sparing of his riches to any man and prodigal of himself. (15) Nevertheless, Proba, the best of wives, obtained this solace for so great a grief as hers, that the urn unites them as equals. Happy, alas too happy, was she, joined to so worthy a man while alive and worthy of the same tomb.

## (ii) Letter of Symmachus

---

Document 86: I.57 (about 383)

Symmachus to Probus
    Having observed both your occupations and the haste of the courier I produce what, for the present, seems sufficient for rewarding friendship. At another time I might not be deprived of your indulgence and the effort of a longer letter. Only may the gods grant what we long for, and keep the safety of the empire on a solid footing! Then will my good-will be more prompt both for writing what you freely accept and in reading what, with unoccupied spirit, you write back. Farewell.

---

# (E) AMBROSE

Ambrose, the son of a Praetorian Prefect of Gaul, moved straight from an administrative post as governor (*consularis*) of Aemilia and Liguria (N. Italy) to the episcopate of Milan, to which he was forcibly elected in 374. He was a prominent opponent of the Arian heresy, both as a legacy from the previous bishop, Auxentius, and as the doctrine of Valentinian's mother, Justina, whose attempt to take over a basilica he successfully resisted in 386. His political activity included an embassy to the usurper Maximus, his successful intervention over the Altar of Victory and his humiliation of the emperor Theodosius over the massacre of Thessalonica in 391. He developed and popularized allegorical methods of biblical exegesis and was an important influence on both Augustine and Paulinus of Nola. He is said to have introduced hymn-singing into the western churches for the first time.[34]

## Letters of Symmachus

---

Document 87: III.30 (before 397)

Symmachus to Ambrose
    You have freely granted many favours to my friend Sallustius.[35]
Add now what remains so that I too may be thought to have a share

---

34.  The standard work on Ambrose remains F. Homes-Dudden, *The Life and Times of Saint Ambrose*, Oxford 1935.
35.  For details: 'Sallustius 4', *PLRE* I, p. 797. He was Prefect of the City of Rome in 387 and involved in the construction of the basilica of St Paul outside the

in your kindness. His additional requests are conveyed by the bearer of this letter, as I considered it superfluous to write them down. The testimony of the spoken word is a more suitable medium for conveying business matters.

## Document 88: III.31 (before 397)

Symmachus to Ambrose
May I repeat my request on behalf of Sallustius who is my friend and, as you have declared yourself, has also been under your protection for some time. It is not that I am afraid of your abandoning your care of him through forgetfulness, as it is a feature of your steadfast character that you carry out faithfully requests made of you, but the welfare of a friend makes constant demands on my concern, and for those hard-pressed a single commendation is not enough. Although you [already] have it firmly in mind I am advising you of it a second time. Speed in performing this favour on your part will be better, lest I be obliged to remind you of it more often.

## Document 89: III.32 (before 397)

Symmachus to Ambrose
Those praiseworthy gentlemen, my brothers Dorotheus and Septimius,[36] have arrived together with a single letter of yours. I felt it my sacred duty to gain a double advantage from it, so that you might be the richer from their twofold performance of duty, and they both profit as individuals from the distinction of the testimonials that is their due. For although our brother Dorotheus already has your confidence, I nevertheless desire that the preference accorded him by my high opinion may raise him yet higher in your favour, which I have no doubt will be the case, since the affection of a noble heart is always able to grow stronger whenever stimulated by kindnesses.

## Document 90: III.33 (395?)

Symmachus to Ambrose
Although I believe that my previous letter, in which I asked that

Walls (S. Paolo fuori le Mura). For the construction of the basilica, its dedication in 391 and its later completion, see A. Chastagnol, 'Sur quelques documents rélatifs à la basilique de Saint-Paul-hors-les-murs', *Mélanges André Piganiol* I, Paris 1966, pp. 421–37.
36. Dorotheus and Septimius are otherwise unknown.

you should shield my good friend Marcianus[37] from injustice, has been delivered to you, I feel it incumbent upon me not to refrain from a second petition, so that a double entreaty will testify to the desperate plight of a gentleman entangled in the enmity deriving from the time of the usurper. I therefore urge you again to protect my friend whose slender means, arising from his personal rectitude, are insufficient to enable him to pay off the price of the grain, a sum that the kindness of the emperor has already reduced for many officials of that time. It will therefore be easier for you to gain your request when the support afforded his case by your own worth is supplemented by the precedent supplied by others. Farewell.

## Document 91: III.34 (392-3)

Symmachus to Ambrose
    My brother Magnillus,[38] having held the Vicariate of Africa with great distinction both in the public and private spheres according to the witness of everyone, is now, like the poet Naevius,[39] detained in his province by a variety of obstacles. You are acquainted with the balanced judgement and other good qualities of this excellent man, qualities through which he won your regard too when he was in charge of Liguria, for which reason it is a waste of effort to praise what is already known to you. Therefore I earnestly request of you that when you learn the reasons for his being delayed from the bearer of this letter, you will see fit to lodge a sincere plea for his return, so that he may at last be restored to his homeland and exchange his unjust and protracted stay abroad for the peace he so desires.

## Document 92: III.35 (before 397)

Symmachus to Ambrose
    It is a matter of experience that those needing help resort to reliable patronage. One such man is Eusebius[40] who, having slipped

37. On Marcianus: 'Marcianus 14', *PLRE* I, pp. 555-6 and for his proconsulship of Africa under Eugenius which gave rise to the circumstances outlined in this letter see Document 50, p. 82.
38. Magnillus was Vicar of Africa at the time of Eugenius' usurpation when Symmachus was waiting for him to return for the quaestorian games of his son Memmius. However, Magnillus was detained in Africa, as referred to here. See 'Magnillus', *PLRE* I, p. 533.
39. Naevius (second century BC) wrote tragedies, comedies and an epic on the First Punic War. Fragments of them survive. The point of Symmachus' comparison is that Naevius was exiled to Africa where he died at Utica.
40. Eusebius is impossible to identify with any certainty.

up through an error of youth and been condemned by a court, now begs that most effective of remedies, the imperial pardon. But, to speed the time when the fulfilment of his desire may smile upon him, he requested that his hopes and petition should be placed in your hands; his plea, in brief, is that by a reversal of the judgement he may heal the wound to his reputation.

---

## Document 93: III.36 (before 397)

Symmachus to Ambrose
My son Caecilianus,[41] a most distinguished man and now administrator of the corn supply for our common fatherland [i.e. Rome], has learned from a reliable source that his adversary at law, named Piratas, or his agent, has strong hopes of your support. I said that you were not in the habit of involving yourself in lawsuits about money. He, however, as is the way with men afflicted with excessive and pointless worry, has asked of me letters suitable for your holy character. I did not deny him my help as what he asked was easy and reasonable. This, in short, is the message I was asked to convey: do not, I pray, allow any recourse to be hoped for from your justice against a Roman citizen who is both absent and confined by public cares. There are laws, tribunals of justice and magistrates which the plaintiff may employ without violation to your conscience. Farewell.

---

## Document 94: III.37 (before 397)

Symmachus to Ambrose
Dusarius,[42] a most distinguished man, who has rightly achieved the highest rank among professors of medicine, desires that his kinsman and namesake be recommended to your patronage at my request. I am glad to gratify a man very close to me so that, by one and the same means, I can pay my respects to you, by wishing you good health, and also do him a favour. Be kind enough, then, to take care of this man recommended to you, while bestowing on me a substitute for personal contact with you. Farewell.

---

41.  Caecilianus was Prefect of the corn supply in 397 and later Vicar (404) and Praetorian Prefect of Italy (409). See 'Caecilianus 1', PLRE II, pp. 244-5.
42.  Dusarius was a famous doctor at Rome at the end of the fourth century. See 'Dusarius', PLRE I, p. 275.

# Bibliographical Note

## 1. Sources

The most comprehensive **collection of documents** in translation
bearing on the issues outlined in this book is J. Stevenson, *Creeds,
Councils and Controversies: Documents Illustrative of the History
of the Church A.D. 337-461* (London 1972). For a full presentation
of all relevant legislation see P. Coleman-Norton, *Roman State and
Christian Church* (London 1966) — vols 1 and 2 cover the fourth
century. For the period of Constantine, J. Stevenson, *A New
Eusebius: Documents Illustrative of the History of the Church to
A.D. 337* (London 1957). The standard sourcebooks for the Roman
empire contain a few relevant documents but are most useful for
the social and cultural setting of religious controversies: A. H. M.
Jones, *A History of Rome through the Fifth Century*, vol. 2 (London 1970) and N. Lewis and M. Reinhold, *Roman Civilization*,
vol. 2 (New York 1966). Of more direct use for the fourth century
is the collection of documents with French translation in A. Chastagnol, *Le Bas-Empire* (Paris 1972). The Theodosian Code is
translated in full by C. Pharr and others, *The Theodosian Code
and the Sirmondian Constitutions* (Princeton 1952).

The standard **translations** of Ammianus Marcellinus, Claudian
and Prudentius, along with selections from the letters of Augustine
and Jerome as well as Augustine's *Confessions* and *City of God*,
and Eusebius' *Church History* are in the Loeb Classical Library.
Selections from Ausonius, Claudian and Prudentius are translated
in *The Last Poets of Imperial Rome* in Penguin Classics. Also
in Penguin Classics are Eusebius' *Church History* and Augustine's
*Confessions*. Zosimus is translated by J. Buchanan and H. Davis,
*Zosimus, Historia Nova* (San Antonio 1967), while the works of
Lactantius are translated in *The Ante-Nicene Fathers*, vol. 7 (trans.
A. Roberts and J. Donaldson).

The **Church historians** are available in the series *A Select
Library of Nicene and Post-Nicene Fathers*, 2nd series (ed. P.
Schaff), 1890-1900, repr. 1952-6, vols 2 (Socrates, Sozomen) and
3 (Theodoret, Rufinus). The works of Ambrose are translated in
the Second Series of the *Nicene and Post-Nicene Fathers*, vol. 10,
as well as in the series *Fathers of the Church* (Catholic University
of America, Washington D.C.). The ongoing series *Ancient Christian Writers* contains the works of Paulinus of Nola (*Letters*, trans.
P. G. Walsh, vols 35 and 36), Arnobius (trans. G. McCracken, vols

* Denotes paperback.

7 and 8), Minucius Felix (trans. G. Clarke, vol. 39) and Firmicus Maternus, *The Error of the Pagan Religions* (trans. C. Forbes, vol. 37). For the *relationes* of Symmachus there is the translation by R. H. Barrow, *Prefect and Emperor: The Relationes of Symmachus A.D. 384* (Oxford 1973). There is no English translation of the letters although the French version (Books I and II only so far) by J. P. Callu, *Symmaque, Lettres* (Budé) t.1. (Paris 1972) is a great service. For particular individuals reference must be made to *PLRE* I and II.

## 2. Background

Two short introductions to the fourth century are G. Downey, *The Late Roman Empire* (New York 1969) and P. Brown, *The World of Late Antiquity* (London 1971). More detailed are A. Piganiol, *L'empire chrétien*, 2nd edn (Paris 1972), E. Stein, *Histoire du Bas-Empire*, 2nd edn (Paris 1959) and J. Matthews, *Western Aristocracies and Imperial Court A.D. 364-425* (Oxford 1975) while for the whole social and administrative framework of late Roman society: A. H. M. Jones, *The Later Roman Empire* (Oxford 1964). Of the **histories of the Church** the best introductions are W. Frend, *The Early Church* (Philadelphia 1966) and H. Chadwick, *The Early Church* (*Pelican History of the Church*, vol. 1, Harmondsworth 1967). More detailed studies are H. Lietzmann, *A History of the Early Church*, vols 3 and 4 (London 1953) and J. R. Palanque, G. Bardy and P. de Labriolle, *De la paix constantinienne à la mort de Théodose* (*Histoire de l'Eglise* t. III, ed. A. Fliche and V. Martin, Paris 1936) translated into English by E. Messenger (London 1949).

Specific studies of the **cultural background** of the pagan/ Christian debate are: C. Cochrane, *Christianity and Classical Culture*, rev. edn (New York 1944, repr. 1966), and the essays edited by A. Momigliano in *The Conflict between Paganism and Christianity in the Fourth Century* (Oxford 1963). Among older works, G. Boissier, *La fin du paganisme*, 5th edn (Paris 1907), S. Dill, *Roman Society in the Last Century of the Western Empire* (London 1898, repr. New York 1958) and the new updated translation of J. Geffcken, *The Last Days of Graeco-Roman Paganism* (Amsterdam 1978) remain indispensable. For the earlier fourth century see D. Bowder, *The Age of Constantine and Julian* (London 1978) and for the reign of Julian in particular: R. Browning, *The Emperor Julian* (London 1976) and G. Bowersock, *Julian the Apostate* (London 1978). On the central religious issues of the reigns of Gratian, Valentinian II and Theodosius see S. L. Greenslade, *Church and State from Constantine to Theodosius* (London 1954) and N. King,

*Theodosius the Great and the Establishment of Christianity* (London 1961).

Particular studies of **individuals** involved in the fourth-century debates are: F. Homes-Dudden, *The Life and Times of St. Ambrose*, 2 vols (Oxford 1935); J.-R. Palanque, *St. Ambroise et l'empire romain* (Paris 1933); J. A. McGeachy, *Quintus Aurelius Symmachus and the Senatorial Aristocracy of the West* (Diss., Chicago 1942); R. Klein, *\*Symmachus: Eine tragische Gestalt des ausgehenden Heidentums* (Darmstadt 1972); A. Lippold, *\*Theodosius der Grosse und seine Zeit* (Stuttgart 1968); P. Brown, *\*Augustine of Hippo* (London 1967) and J. N. D. Kelly, *Jerome* (London 1975).

The standard general accounts of **Roman religion** are K. Latte, *Römische Religionsgeschichte* (Munich 1960) and G. Wissowa, *Religion und Kultus der Römer* (Munich 1912). Particularly useful works in English are: R. Ogilvie, *\*The Romans and their Gods* (London 1969); J. Ferguson, *The Religions of the Roman Empire* (London 1970); W. Liebeschuetz, *Continuity and Change in Roman Religion* (Oxford 1979) and A. D. Nock, *\*Conversion* (Oxford 1933, repr. 1972). On the various Eastern cults celebrated at Rome: M. Vermaseren, *Cybele and Attis, the Myth and the Cult* (London 1977); F. Cumont, *\*The Mysteries of Mithra* (New York 1903, repr. 1956) and *\*Oriental Religions in Roman Paganism* (New York 1911, repr. 1956).

# Glossary of Deities and Rites at Rome

(Those deities and ceremonies referred to frequently in the documents are marked with an asterisk. Particularly relevant document numbers are given in bold type.)

Acheron:
: One of the five rivers surrounding the underworld, Hades. The souls of the dead were required to bathe in it or cross it. (**50**)

Adonis:
: The handsome favourite of Venus* who, while hunting, was killed by Vulcan* disguised as a boar. He was mourned in an annual ceremony. (**50, 52**)

Anubis:
: The hunter who found the scattered remnants of the body of Osiris* and brought them to Isis*. He was represented with a dog's head in the Isis ceremonies. (**50**)

Apollo:
: The god of fine arts and reputed originator of music, poetry and eloquence.

Asclepius:
: The ancient god of medicine whose cult was transferred from Epidaurus to Rome; usually represented as a snake. (**3**)

Attis:
: The fruit of the almond tree of Agdistis impregnated the daughter of Sangarius, so he tried to kill her and expose the baby. Cybele*, however, intervened to save him. When the baby (Attis) grew up Cybele fell in love with him and sent him mad as a punishment, whereupon he castrated himself under a pine tree. In his annual festival (15-28 March) a pine tree was carried through the city to the Palatine on 22 March. On 24 March, the *dies sanguinis* (day of blood), the funeral of Attis was celebrated with the flagellation of his eunuch priests (*galli*) (**55, 67**). The Hilaria or resurrection of Attis was held on the following day (25 March) and the festival culminated in a *taurobolium* at the Vatican Phrygianum on 28 March. (**50, 55, 67**)

Bacchus:
: The Greek god of wine, Dionysus, whose cult was symbolized by orgiastic excess. (**47, 50**)

Bellona:
: The Romans identified Bellona with the Cappadocian Mother-Goddess, Ma. She had a temple in the Campus Martius and her Asiatic ritual involved her priests in slashing themselves and sprinkling their blood over the statue. (**50, 57**)

Berecynthian Mother:
   Another name for Cybele*, taken from Mt Berecynthus in Phrygia, the centre of her worship. (50)

Castor and Pollux:
   The Greek Dioscuri, who had a temple in the Roman Forum, were the sons of Zeus and Leda. Castor was a horse-tamer and mortal, Pollux a boxer and immortal. (37)

Ceres:
   The ancient Italian corn goddess, identified with the Greek Demeter who searched for her daughter Persephone (Proserpine*) whom Pluto had abducted.

Cora:
   Another name for Proserpine*, daughter of Ceres*. (65)

Cupid:
   God of love, son of Venus* and Mars*. (50)

Cybele:
   The Great Mother goddess from Pessinus in Asia. She was sleeping, in the shape of a rock, when Zeus (Jupiter*) attempted to rape her. Seed was spilt on the ground and a monster named Agdistis was born. Dionysus (Bacchus*) tried to drug him and tied his genitals to a tree. On awakening Agdistis castrated himself. An almond tree sprang from the blood and the daughter of Sangarius, the river god, picked fruit from it which impregnated her and so Attis* was born. The cult of Cybele was introduced into Rome in 204 BC when the sacred black stone of the goddess was brought from Mt Ida. Her annual festival, the *Megalensia*, was held from 4 to 10 April. (3, 5, 47, 53) She was associated with the rites of Attis and the ritual washing of her statue in the Almo was held on 27 March. (41)

Dodona:
   An oracle at a sanctuary of Zeus in Epirus. Responses came from the sacred oak tree.

Eleusinian Mysteries:
   A secret cult at Eleusis in Greece, associated with the myth of Ceres*.

Fauns:
   Rural deities represented as having legs, feet and ears of goats, and the remainder of the body human.

Flora:
   The Italian goddess of flowering plants and fertility in general, an aspect of the Great Mother*. Her annual feast, the *Floralia* (28 April-3 May), included licentious mimes and games. (50, 56)

Genius:
   Attendant spirit of each man, often likened to a guardian angel, and family. It was later extended to cities, corporations and other places.

Great Mother:
A classical feminine archetype whose aspects are manifested in various ways in Isis*, Cybele* and Demeter. She is known at Rome as the *Magna Mater* and the *Megalensia** was her festival.

Hecate:
An underworld goddess, daughter of Zeus, whose secret rites were centred at Aegina. (**66, 67**)

Iacchus:
Son of Ceres*, associated with the Eleusinian mysteries*, usually identified with Liber/Bacchus*.

Isis:
The mother of Horus, sister and wife of Osiris*. Osiris' body was put in a coffin by Set and carried off to Syria. Isis wandered in search of the body but no sooner had he been found than Set stole it again. This time he completely dismembered it and Isis recovered all the pieces, except the genitals, with the help of Anubis*. The annual Isis ceremonial was quite spectacular with hymns and sacred dances presided over by her shaven-headed priests. Isis is normally depicted carrying her rattle (*sistrum*) and a container (*situla*) of Nile water. (**47, 50, 51, 54**)

Janus:
The ancient Latin God of beginnings and the doorway (*ianua*) and was therefore portrayed as two-headed, looking forward and backward. (**5, 22, 56**)

Juno:
The Greek Hera, wife and sister of Jupiter*.

Jupiter:
The Greek Zeus. The chief of all gods, born in Crete, the son of Saturn* and husband of Juno* and Ceres*. His temple on the Capitol was shared with Juno* and Minerva* and the three were known together as the 'Capitoline Triad' which came to symbolize Rome. Jupiter is accused of incest. He frequently changed shape to fulfil his lustful purposes. (**4, 49, 50, 71**)

Lar/Lares:
Originally deities of the farm land and later of the house. Later still, they were expanded to cover the state in general. (**5, 50**)

Liber:
Another name for Bacchus*. (**65, 67**)

Lupercal:
A small cave beneath the Palatine where on the *Lupercalia* (15 February) goats and a dog were sacrificed. Then the leaders of two teams of *Luperci*, normally young aristocrats, were smeared with the sacrificial blood and raced around the Palatine beating any intruders with goat-skin whips. (**5**)

Mars:
   An ancient Italian god, the son of Jupiter* and Juno*. The Greek Ares,
   god of war. (**49, 50**)

Megalensia:
   Festival of the Great Mother*, 4-10 April. There was a procession
   of the goddess in her chariot drawn by lions and accompanied by her
   brightly dressed eunuch priests to the music of tambourine, flute and
   cymbals. Plays were performed in the theatre on the Palatine and there
   were games in the Circus. There was a special common meal (*lectister-
   nium*) where aristocratic families brought dishes of *moretum* (white
   cheese and spices) for Cybele*, set aside on a special couch.

Mercury:
   The son of Jupiter* and Maia who was messenger of the gods and
   conducted the souls of the dead to Hades. He presided over orators
   and merchants.

Minerva:
   The goddess of wisdom, war and the liberal arts who sprang, fully
   grown, from the head of Jupiter*.

Mithras:
   A mediator with the Persian sun-god Ahura-Mazda, whose first creation had been a wild bull. The bull was captured by Mithras and
   dragged off to a cave. It later escaped but Mithras found it, grasped
   its head and pulled it back and plunged his dagger into the bull. This
   is the scene so frequently depicted. The cult of Mithras, who became
   assimilated to the sun-god in Roman times, was a personal religion,
   especially popular among the Roman army.

Neptune:
   Greek Poseidon, god of the sea, normally depicted with a trident.
   (**50**)

Numa:
   The second king of Rome who was traditionally responsible for
   establishing the laws and rituals of traditional Roman religion.

Osiris:
   An Egyptian king, brother and husband of Isis*, who brought civilization to his people.

Paeonian Serpent:
   Another name for Asclepius. The 'Paeonii' were the sons of Paeon, the
   ancient god of medicine, and later sons of Asclepius*. (**3**)

Pan:
   The god of shepherds, huntsmen, and country folk. He was depicted
   as having two small horns on his head while his legs, tail and feet
   were those of a goat.

Penates:
   These were the guardian spirits of a family, the chief private cult of
   every household.

Phoebus:
Another name for Apollo*, the god of fine arts and reputed originator of music, poetry and eloquence.

Proserpine:
The Greek Persephone (Cora*), daughter of Zeus (Jupiter*) and Demeter (Ceres*). While gathering flowers she was abducted by Pluto. When Ceres* discovered this she demanded that Pluto be punished while she searched for her daughter. (50)

Rumor:
The last child of Earth. She was swift-footed with an eye under every feather and an ear, tongue and voice for every eye. (2)

Saturn:
King of the universe and father of Jupiter*, identified with the Greek Kronos. It was custom to offer human sacrifices on his altar until the intervention of Hercules. His annual feast, the Saturnalia, began on 17 December. (5, 49, 50, 52, 56)

Satyrs:
These were demi-gods, similar in appearance to the Fauns*. (50)

Serapis:
One of the Egyptian deities, supposed to be the same as Osiris*. He was a healer of the sick and worker of miracles who spoke in dreams. (50, 53)

Sibyl:
A prophetic woman who lived in a cave at Cumae and who sold to the last king of Rome a collection of oracles, known as the Sibylline books. (3, 6, 50)

Sterculus:
A rural divinity who invented the art of manuring lands. (5)

Taurobolium:
A rite associated with both Mithras* and Cybele* whereby an initiate, standing in a pit, was drenched with the blood of a bull sacrificed on a grid above him. (54, 67)

Tritonia:
Another name for Minerva* derived from her worship near lake Tritonis. The head of the Gorgon (Medusa) was depicted on shields to ward off enemies. (3, 56)

Venus:
The goddess of love and beauty, married to Vulcan* and enamoured of Adonis*, sometimes identified with the sea-goddess Galatea.

Vesta:
A Roman hearth goddess, prominent in family worship. She had a sanctuary in the forum where burnt an eternal flame.

Vestal Virgins:
   These were normally six Vestals who remained virgins for thirty years.
   Candidates were aged six to ten years and were selected by the *pon-
   tifex maximus*. They tended the cult of Vesta*. (**41, 58, 59, 77**)

Vulcan:
   An ancient Italian fire-god, son of Jupiter* and Juno*, who broke his
   leg when thrown out of heaven and was lame thereafter. His annual
   festival, the *Vulcanalia*, was held on 23 August.

# Index of Documents

The editions cited are those used for the translations. The number of the document in translation is given in bold type.

Ambrose,
    *De obitu Theodosii* 1, 2, 4, 6, 33, 39, 56 (**48**) (ed. O. Faller, *CSEL* 73)

Ambrose,
    *De obitu Valentiniani* 19-20, 52, 55 (**43**) (ed. O. Faller, *CSEL* 73)

Ambrose,
    *Epistulae* XVII (**39**), XVIII (**41**), LVII (**44**) (ed. R. Klein, *Der Streit um den Victoriaaltar*, Darmstadt 1972, and *PL* 16)

Ambrosiaster (Ps-Augustine),
    *Quaestiones veteris et novi testamenti* 114 (**56**) (ed. A. Souter, *CSEL* 50)

Ammianus Marcellinus,
    *Res Gestae* XIV.6.3-6 (**1**), XVI.10.13-17 (**2**), XIX.10.1, 4 (**37**) (ed. C. Clark)

Anonymous,
    *Carmen contra paganos* (**50**) (ed. A. Riese, *Anthologia Latina*, 2nd edn, I.4, pp. 20-5)

*Corpus Inscriptionum Latinarum*
    VI.102 (**62**), 1699 (**57**), 1751 (**81**), 1753 (**82**), 1754 (**84**), 1755 (**83**), 1756 (**85**), 1777 (**63**), 1778 (**64**), 1779 (**67**), 1780 (**65**), 1782 (**74**), 2145 (**66**)

Claudian,
    *De consulatu Stilichonis* III.130-73 (**3**) (ed. T. Birt, *MGH AA* X)

Claudian,
    *De sexto consulatu Honorii* 39-52 (**4**) (ed. T. Birt, *MGH AA* X)

*Codex Theodosianus*
    IV.7.1 (**14**); IX.16.2 (**15**), 3 (**16**), 4 (**24**), 7 (**25**), 8 (**27**), 9 (**28**); XVI.1.1 (**28**), 2.2 (**12**), 4 (**13**), 5 (**18**); XVI.10.2 (**19**), 3 (**20**), 4 (**21**), 5 (**22**), 6 (**23**), 7 (**29**), 8 (**30**), 10 (**32**), 12 (**33**), 14 (**34**), 15 (**35**), 16 (**36**) (ed. T. Mommsen and E. Meyer)

Eusebius,
    *Historia Ecclesiastica* X.5.15-17 (**9**), 6.1-3 (**10**), 7.2 (**11**) (ed. E. Schwartz, *GCS* 9.1, 2, 3)

Firmicus Maternus,
    *De errore profanarum religionum* 18, 21, 22 (**55**) (ed. K. Halm, *CSEL* 2)

Lactantius,
    *De mortibus persecutorum* 34 (**7**), 48.2-6 (**8**) (ed. S. Brandt and G. Laubmann, *CSEL* 27.2)

Paulinus of Milan,
*Vita Ambrosii* 26 (**42**) (*PL* 14)

Paulinus of Nola,
*Carmen* XIX.45-75 (**6**), 84-158 (**53**) (ed. W. Hartel, *CSEL* 30)

Prudentius,
*Peristephanon* II.1-20, 413-536, 553-64 (**5**); X.1007-50 (**54**), (ed. P. Cunningham, *CCh* 126)

Prudentius,
*Contra Symmachum* I.1-41, 408-16, 442-642 (**47**); II.17-38, 270-334, 640-772 (**49**) (ed. P. Cunningham, *CCh* 126)

Pseudo-Cyprian,
*Carmen ad senatorem* (**51**) (ed. W. Hartel, *CSEL* 3.3, pp. 302 ff. and 23.1, pp. 227 ff.)

Pseudo-Paulinus,
*Carmen* XXXII.1-164 (**52**) (ed. W. Hartel, *CSEL* 40, pp. 329 ff.)

Rufinus of Aquileia,
*Historia Ecclesiastica* XI.31-3 (**45**) (ed. E. Schwartz and T. Mommsen, *GCS* 9.3)

Symmachus,
*Relatio* III (**40**) (ed. O. Seeck, *MGH AA* VI)

Symmachus,
*Epistulae* I.46 (**68**), 47 (**69**), 48 (**70**), 49 (**71**), 50 (**72**), 51 (**73**), 57 (**86**), 64 (**61**); II.7 (**75**), 34 (**76**), 36 (**77**), 50 (**78**), 53 (**79**), 59 (**80**); III.30 (**87**), 31 (**88**), 32 (**89**), 33 (**90**), 34 (**91**), 35 (**92**), 36 (**93**), 37 (**94**); IX.108 (**58**), 147 (**59**), 148 (**60**) (ed. O. Seeck, *MGH AA* VI)

Zosimus,
*Historia Nova* IV.3.2-3 (**38**), 59.1-3 (**46**) (ed. L. Mendelssohn)

# General Index